*Romantic Opera and Literary Form*

## ABOUT
# QUANTUM
# BOOKS

QUANTUM, THE UNIT OF
EMITTED ENERGY. A QUANTUM
BOOK IS A SHORT STUDY
DISTINCTIVE FOR THE AUTHOR'S
ABILITY TO OFFER A RICHNESS OF
DETAIL AND INSIGHT WITHIN
ABOUT ONE HUNDRED PAGES
OF PRINT. SHORT ENOUGH TO BE
READ IN AN EVENING AND
SIGNIFICANT ENOUGH
TO BE A BOOK.

Peter Conrad

# Romantic Opera and Literary Form

University of California Press

*Berkeley · Los Angeles · London*

University of California Press
Berkeley and Los Angeles, California

University of California Press, Ltd.
London, England

First Paperback Printing 1981
ISBN 0-520-04508-4
Library of Congress Catalog Card Number: 76-14312
Printed in the United States of America

1 2 3 4 5 6 7 8 9

Add
4193

# Contents

# List of Illustrations

# Acknowledgments

The opportunity to write this book I owe to the friendly initiative of Ted Schuller, and in working on it I have benefited, I hope, from the critical advice of W. J. McClung and Doris Kretschmer of the University of California Press and U. C. Knoepflmacher of Berkeley. Earlier versions of some paragraphs appeared in articles contributed to the *Times Literary Supplement,* and I must thank the Editor, John Gross, for the chance to write them in the first place and for permission to rewrite them here. Quotations from the work of W. H. Auden are printed by permission of Edward Mendelson of Yale University.

The writing was completed at Princeton, where during 1975 and 1976 I was Hodder Fellow. I have to thank the Council of the Humanities for this award and the Governing Body of Christ Church, Oxford, for granting me leave to accept it. Dr. Waltraud Neuwirth of the Österreichisches Museum für angewandte Kunst, Michael Bronson and Johanna Fiedler of the Metropolitan Opera, New York, and Georgette Rostand of the Théâtre National de l'Opéra, Paris, were most helpful; in Princeton, Tom Roche and Walt Litz were immensely kind. The wisdom, wit, and generosity of Paul and Betty Fussell enriched my year in America, and, I should like to hope, this book.

# Introduction

"Music–drama," the slogan Wagner attached to his own reformed version of opera, has gained through him a critical currency it never deserved and ever since has bedevilled understanding of opera and its relation to literary form. The virtue of "music–drama" as a slogan is exactly its disqualification as a critical term, for its efficacy depends on its adroit begging of two questions which the present book reopens.

Neatly compounding music and drama, Wagner's portmanteau is thus saved from investigating the exact nature of their alliance. My argument is that music and drama are dubious, even antagonistic, partners and that opera's actual literary analogue is the novel. Drama is limited to the exterior life of action, and romanticism increasingly deprecates both the tedious willfulness of action and the limits of the form which transcribes it. The novel, in contrast, can explore the interior life of motive and desire and is naturally musical because mental. It traces the motions of thought, of which music is an image. Opera is more musical novel than musical drama.

The second question which Wagner's term slides over is whether drama is the only literary form to bear upon opera. This book shows opera employing a variety of literary forms—epic, romance, allegory, and the psychological novel—of which drama is perhaps the least significant. "Drama" owes its immortality as a caption to its gradual evacuation of meaning: its convenience is its vacancy. During the nineteenth century, it degenerated from a term classifying form to one rhetorically approving of content. By now, to assert that opera is or ought to be drama says nothing about its literary means: it means no more than to say that good operas are, in the word's vulgar sense, "dramatic." That can mean that they are psychologically plausible or merely that they are excitingly eventful, but either way it describes content while pretending to define form.

Forgotten inside the slogan there is, however, a reference to a certain literary form. When critics like Shaw refer to the Wagnerian ideal of music-drama, they mean by drama the intellectualized morality plays of Ibsen, in which characters have no existence beyond their opinions and action is the dialectic of their opposed ideas. There is, as the first chapter of this book will argue, a single operatic example of this form, *Das Rheingold*; and it is, aptly, Wagner's least operatic work. While this notion of dramatic form prevails, not even Shakespeare may be counted as a dramatist. Shaw dismisses him as too hasty, improvisatory, and convention-ridden. Shakespeare's characters are not the judicial exemplars of motive and accountability which drama demands: they are rebellious and undetermined, truculent in comedy, indecorous in tragedy. Nor are the actions in Shakespeare's plays those proper to drama: instead of evidentially unravelling a character's moral or ideological potentiality, they adhere to the etiquette of inherited plots, which the characters are often encouraged to flout. Hamlet and Falstaff, two figures important in this book, do so: the one absents himself from, the other impudently parodies, the actions of the plays they find themselves incongruously assigned to.

Though Shaw is wrong to be so absurdly severe about Shakespeare's deviations from drama, his literary instinct is right: Shakespeare is not, in Wagner's or Ibsen's or Shaw's sense, a dramatist. Shakespeare recurs throughout this book, and always in opposition to drama. In the first two chapters, Berlioz and Verdi remake his tragicomic history in the semblance of a nineteenth-century novel of social destinies. In the third chapter, the escape of Shakespeare's restless characters from drama into novelistic sequels is the model for the various speculative continuations of *Die Zauberflöte*. In the fourth chapter, Hofmannsthal adduces Shakespeare as a justification for his own version of the musical novel. Shakespeare is in all cases treated as a novelist rather than a dramatist. Anxious to separate Shakespeare from the mercantile taint and tawdry impersonations of the stage, romanticism first rewrites the plays as lyrical poems but then goes on to extend them into novels, meditatively passive and self-exploratory, not fretfully active like drama; music confirms this reinterpretation.

This book has chosen to concentrate on romantic opera because opera is one agency of the invasion of drama by the novel which occurs in the nineteenth century. Shakespeare is virtually a creation of romantic criticism. Though he may not be romantic in himself, he is a cause of romanticism in others. This is also true of Mozart, whose operas have a Shakespearean aptitude for self-transformation. Don Giovanni may be an eighteenth-century hero of ravenous sensibility, but he becomes romantic after the event, successively remade as a dangerous satanist by E. T. A. Hoffmann, a spirit of musical hedonism by Kierkegaard, a revolutionary pamphleteer by Shaw, and, terminally, a victim of psychotherapy by Otto Rank. *Die Zauberflöte* may be flatly rational in its morality, exchanging enchantment for the dour rule of Sarastro, but it too is romantically reinterpreted, as the third chapter describes, by Goethe's metaphysics, Kierkegaard's sexual ethics, Hofmannsthal's allegorical fantasy, and Auden's cheerful updatings.

All these continuations of *Die Zauberflöte* have, however, an indirect or vexed relation to music. Goethe's is an incomplete text for an opera which was never composed, Kierkegaard's is literary criticism, Hofmannsthal's is a novelistic recension of a drama blurred and spoiled by music, Auden's poems are inserted into a translation of Schikaneder's libretto. The treatment of works like these, and of the monologue *Lélio* by Berlioz, or of Salome's excursions through literature, dance, and painting, ought perhaps to be explained in advance. The equivalence between music and words which Wagner's theory of opera as drama assumes is a false compact. Actually the two are more like enemies. Music liquifies words, subduing them into notes; song infects language with an inspired un-reason. Few words can be heard distinctly, and even those many opera-goers prefer not to acknowledge, defending their right to listen to works performed in languages foreign to them because they know that in-comprehension exalts and mystifies. As if in restitu-tion, I have on occasion considered the texts, complex and slighted subjects of study, apart from the music. The cases I have chosen invite such treatment. Berlioz and Wagner correctly believed the literary substance of their operas to be as significant as the music. Verdi and Boïto have in *Falstaff* improved, even redeemed, Shakespeare. The redactions of *Die Zauberflöte* all hope to dignify the text so as to make it worthy of the sol-emn and prophetic music. The correspondence be-tween Strauss and Hofmannsthal reveals the poet maneuvring to preserve his texts from violation by uncomprehending music. Salome at first seeks refuge from words in music, but eventually retreats from music as well.

As the texts are separable from their music, so the romantic idea of opera is to an extent separable from the actuality of operas composed. Hence the discussion in this book of critical theories of opera like those of Heine, Shaw, Symons, d'Annunzio, and Hofmanns-thal, or of para-operatic works like those in the third chapter. The idea of opera, of a chimerical reunion of the arts and specifically of literature's salvation by music, develops through the nineteenth century in vir-tual disregard of actual operatic practice, until works like *Ariadne auf Naxos* or *Capriccio* cease to be operas and become instead disquisitions on the operatic idea. The final pair of chapters describes the fate of the idea, in Hofmannsthal's belated recognition that the musical novel is to be made by the incorporation of music into literature, not the surrender of literature to music, and in Salome's renunciation of both literature and music.

The sequence of the chapters demonstrates the book's two complaints about music-drama, stated at the beginning of this preface. The chapters describe the series of literary forms which support opera; but each of these forms is consciously allied with the novel against drama.

Epic and romance are reconstituted in the nineteenth century as precursors of the novel. They record the evolution of the heroic individual who at last divests himself of his heroism in the realistic novel. Both Wagner's *Ring* in its backward progress from the epic calamity of *Götterdämmerung* to the leisurely romance of the young Siegfried's search to know the meaning of fear, and Berlioz's *Les Troyens* in its migration from the epic doom of Troy to the idyllic romance of Carthage, re-enact this evolution. Each grows from static, embattled epic into wayfaring, erotically adventurous romance, and each acknowledges its antique forms as heroic extensions of the novel. Wagner's epic is a novel in code. Nibelheim is (as Shaw pointed out) a manufacturing town, Valhalla (as Wieland Wagner understood) the jagged skyline of Wall Street. Berlioz likewise transforms Virgil's mythic history into an unclassical conflict, familiar from the nineteenth-century novel, between pitiless public obligations and private emotional loyalties, between the different realms which Ruskin called kings' treasuries and queens' gardens.

The individual first releases himself from service to the epic community in the digressive freedom of romance. Allegory reinterprets the perils and obstructions of the romance quest as moral portents, signs corresponding to the stations of a spiritual progress; the novel in its turn converts the romance's succession of adventures into the streamy continuity of consciousness. Self-consciousness turns Shakespeare's characters, in the romantic view, from dramatic activists into lyrically irresolute monologuists who belong in a novel which concentrates on recording their troubled sense of themselves, not what they do. In drama, Macbeth is an unscrupulous hell-hound; but in the lyrical novel, which overhears his debates with himself, he retains an agonizingly delicate apprehension of his crimes as crises of will and spiritual temptations, not crass, gruesome deeds. Hence romantic composers tend to adapt the plays most successfully not as operas but as symphonic poems, in which characters can meditate musically without the interference of action or the intermediary of words. The antagonism between drama and the novel recurs in the various novelistic efforts to justify the episodic drama of *Die Zauberflöte,* and in Hofmannsthal's alternative versions of his own *Zauberflöte, Die Frau ohne Schatten.*

Hofmannsthal's critical essays, discussed in the fourth chapter, dismiss drama and annex the novel to music because the novel is a private, self-soliloquizing

form. Hofmannsthal defines the novel psychologically: verismo artists, and Strauss himself in the years
after his collaboration with Hofmannsthal, make the
mistake of interpreting the novel literally, as a form
specializing in prosaic detail and flat materialism. As
the later part of the fourth chapter shows, they demor-
alize opera because they leave no excuse for music. In
the interests of realism they are driven to a reinforce-
ment of convention: they have to write operas about
opera-singers, like Tosca, because only a tempera-
mental soprano can in all conscience be permitted to
behave operatically.

The final chapter derives from the work which immediately preceded Strauss's partnership with Hofmannsthal, *Salome*. It describes not a form but a
character who traverses all forms and discloses their
limitations, who is liberated from Wilde's drama by
music but goes on to unfold aspects of herself in forms
which lead beyond opera and literature: the symphonic poem, dance, and painting.

# 1. Operatic Epic and Romance

Epic and romance are the narrative forms which divide between them the early history of literature and which record the gradual emergence of the heroic individual. As literature moves into reverse in the nineteenth century, hoping to develop backwards in a quest for its origins, epic and romance are resuscitated and acquire new meanings. This chapter introduces the study of literary form in romantic music by describing the operatic meanings of epic and romance.

In medieval literature, epic is the more primitive form. The epic hero remains subject to a society itself straitened by military necessity, which imposes on him the rigid conformity of the warrior, receding into the ranks of his fellows. Romance is the later form, freeing the individual from the duty of defending his society and granting him the leisure to explore the territory outside it. Heroism has become not only a social but also a personal virtue. The romance hero no longer has charge of an army but rides alone through a perilous landscape, his object not military aggression but a search which is endlessly protracted because its goal is forever retreating into the distance. Jowett's mocking question to Rossetti in Beerbohm's cartoon—"And what were they going to do with the Grail when they found it?"—does not arise because the romance hero can never find it. It lies within and behind him, not ahead. Hence, the secrets of Wagner's

Grail knights concern their past, not a future of chivalric accomplishment: Lohengrin's disclosure of his father's name, Parsifal's discovery of his mother's fate.

The nineteenth century makes romance a record of battles not with giants and dragons but with the obstacles which lie in the way of self-discovery. Byron's *Don Juan,* for instance, rescues Mozart's Don Giovanni and makes him a hero of romance. In the opera, the libertine has lost the easy, accommodating ebullience of the romance hero: adventures no longer progress as planned, and his final intransigence thrusts him incongruously into tragedy. But in Byron's comic poem, removed to the unspoiled beginnings of his career, he slides like the itinerant horseman of romance nonchalantly into attachments with the various women who litter his path. Mozart's opera is terminal: its first bars are an announcement of death. Byron's poem is optimistically endless, and in its final stanza even the retributive ghost is unmasked as another erotic victim.

Picaresque infinitude like that of Byron's Juan is a quality of the romance's narrative. Whereas epic deals in completed actions, campaigns fought and decisively won or lost, romance can never be concluded, because the process of experiencing must continue until time itself has a stop. Hence the cyclical structure of medieval romance, in which knights cross paths or adventure in circles, every return home being merely a preparation for another journey. Interlacing and involution like this recur in Wagner's oddly overlapping romance narratives, which reinterpret the medieval tales: Parsifal, whom Lohengrin claims as his father, was in one project for the third act of *Tristan und Isolde* to stray into Tristan's Breton estate of Kareol; the author of the medieval *Parzival,* which Wagner used as a source both for *Lohengrin* and his own *Parsifal,* is a character in *Tannhäuser;* in *Die Meistersinger* Walther acknowledges the influence of another of the contestants at the Wartburg, Walther von der Vogelweide, and Sachs quotes the cautionary example of Isolde and Marke.

The habits of romance are acclimatized to the nineteenth-century novel: such coincidental intrusions of one work on another suggest Balzac's method of allowing the same characters to wander through various volumes of his human comedy. In medieval literature, the collisions have a fortuitous naturalness: all journeys set out from and return to the Grail castle, where the knights are seated as colleagues at the round table. But Wagner forces the connections, imprisoning his characters in relationships in the hope of creating in his work an equivalent to the collectivity of medieval romance, in which anonymous deposits of narrative matter grow together, entangling memories of myth and changed versions of religious ritual. Dante had composed a divine comedy. Balzac humanized it. The romance habit of interlinking places Wagner's chivalric operas midway between Dante's diagram of the spirit and Balzac's secular and mercantile society. Wagner describes the intermediate state between gods and men. Uncertainty of genre makes his works incline in both directions, the divine and the bourgeois, at once: he composes a heroic comedy which defensively parodies itself. The courtly song competition at the Wartburg declines into the auction of Eva to the tradesmen of Nuremberg. Under the patronage of Walther von der Vogelweide, the aristocratic Stolzing appears in dourly proper Nuremberg as if an exile from *Tannhäuser*. Tannhäuser scandalizes the company by the profanity of his song, Walther offends because of technical improprieties. Religious fervour declines, in a later and more materialist state of society, into aesthetic formalism, and the cult now organizes itself as a guild.

Romance becomes the form in which the migratory individual searches for himself, undertaking either the penitential journey from the Hörselberg to Rome and back or the comic journey of self-improvement from Franconia to Nuremberg. Meanwhile, epic in the nineteenth century sets itself to describe a similar self-discovery on the part of society. The romance hero is an innocent introvert, unaware of political vocation; epic deals with his passage from the apprenticeship of private life to the embodiment of a national destiny.

In the confidential letters on the French stage written to August Lewald in 1837, Heine made a similar contrast between the musical forms of Rossini and Meyerbeer. Rossini's music ministers to the delicious idleness of private life, the dreamy connoisseurship of sensation. But Meyerbeer's has in it the din of battle, and it serves those who struggle in the conflicts of their times. Rossini lulls his listeners melodically, Meyerbeer rouses them harmonically. Because Rossini's music is always the expression of a single mind's isolated feeling, melody must predominate in it, being the voice of what Heine calls "isolirten Empfindens," isolated emotion. But in Meyerbeer melody is engulfed in harmony, and for Heine this represents the individual's exemplary submergence in his society, his progress from the sensuous prostration of romance to the communal fate of epic. As he puts it, the melodies are "drowned in the stream of harmonious masses, just as the characteristic feelings of single men are lost in this united feeling of a whole race, and our soul gladly throws itself into this harmonious flood when it is inspired and seized by the joys and sorrows of all mankind, and takes part in the great questions of society."

The change of form is a political conversion, the graduation to a mission: Gurnemanz forces the change on Parsifal, and Sachs prepares Walther for it in his warning about the threatened Holy Roman Empire. While Rossini's music is a survival from the days of the Restoration, when political quarrels receded and individuals basked hedonistically in a new sense of themselves, Heine sees Meyerbeer's operas as music fit for the heady public antagonisms of the Revolution or the Empire. Social rather than individual, Meyerbeer's music rouses men, in the huge choruses of *Robert le Diable* or *Les Huguenots,* from the melodic slumber of private feeling to the harmonious community of partisanship. Rossini retired prematurely into the cultivation of a hearty appetite, sinking into the otiose unselfconsciousness of the body; Meyerbeer took on himself the austere responsibilities of mind, striving towards an idea of himself, and for Heine this ambition is an image of the national self-awareness of "young, great-hearted, cosmopolite Germany . . . which has made all the questions of humanity its own."

Democratizing epic, Meyerbeer rids it of its bellicosity and its heroic authoritarianism. He remakes it on the Westminster model. His art, as Heine interprets it, is an instance of government by consent. Even the borrowings and complimenting of acknowledged masters in *Robert le Diable* are justified as a studious canvassing of the electorate: "He flattered all the caprices of the public, and shook hands right and left with everybody most earnestly, as if he had recognized in music itself the sovereignty of the people, and would found his government on a majority of votes." Rossini on the other hand remains, like all hedonists, an absolute monarch, subjecting the world to his whim.

The epic is an army as well as a parliament. Heine points out that Meyerbeer does have melodies but never permits them to obtrude egotistically; they are disciplined, made to march in time with the whole, whereas in Italian opera melodies are "isolated, I might almost say outlawed, and come out and show themselves like their famous bandits." Meyerbeer's compositions represent the measured tread of troops in rank and file; Rossini's have the vainglorious swagger and irresponsibility of the single Calabrian robber. Wagner remarked that in *Les Huguenots* we hear the same thing we see in a Prussian regiment of guards.

The medieval hero is demobilized from epic to romance; the nineteenth-century hero moves in the opposite direction, and his graduation to epic entails a renunciation of personality, of that subtle psychological indeterminacy which is suggested by romance and which, as the chapter on Hofmannsthal's criticism will explain, defines novelistic as opposed to dramatic character. Heine condemns *Robert le Diable* for its introversion, its moral irresolution and mental restlessness—it is regressive in being too concerned with the mind obstinately self-centred, like Hamlet, and refusing the challenge of political sympathy. *Les Huguenots* overcomes this dubiety and is impersonal, collective, colossal, a work in which the private solicitings of music have given way to a musical architecture which is open to public use.

The specific architectural analogy Heine chooses is a

Gothic cathedral. Throughout the nineteenth century this was an image of art in the service of faith, not doubt, of art as a systematic inventory of the contents of the natural world and an exposition of history, art which had made itself in a long process of evolution rather than owing its existence to a single artist. Because the cathedral proclaimed the notion of an art which was dogmatic and epic, not romantically self-divided and self-communing, it was naturally the object of artistic assaults in a later period: Debussy sinks his cathedral under the sea, Monet makes his molten in a dazzling light, Browning in *The Ring and the Book* enthrones the Pope in a cathedral built to the subversive creed of relativism. But for Heine the image is still safe from such subtle underminings, and he uses it as a declaration of Meyerbeer's skill in construction (the whole is a giant's labour, the details the craftsmanship of an ingenious and unwearying dwarf: Heine's image joins Fafner, Fasolt, and Mime in unlikely collaboration) and his moral solidity. He recalls that a friend had asked him at Amiens why such cathedrals could no longer be built. His reply was, "Men in those days had convictions; we moderns have opinions," and while opinions may make novels or poems they are not foundations for a cathedral. Meyerbeer, however, has convictions.

Heine's praise of Meyerbeer is countered by Wagner's attack on him in *Oper und Drama,* which denies him convictions and accuses him of trading in effects without causes, compiling nuances and contrasts for the scene-shifters. Wagner is closer to the truth. Meyerbeer was guilty of turning the cathedral into a gargantuan shop, mistaking the temple for "la grande boutique," the vast musical emporium of the

Palais Garnier which stands on the street named after Meyerbeer's librettist, Scribe. He represents the nineteenth-century corruption of epic: with his managerial instinct and his concern to keep his shelves stocked with the widest variety of effects, allowing the buying public maximum choice, he turned the past into merchandise and epic into a commodity.

The Palais Garnier was both the factory in which epics were manufactured on a production line and the Crystal Palace in which they were displayed for sale. It imposed an industrial standardization on its composers, insisting for example on the insertion of ballets in the same way that a machine must flaunt a novel gadget, and punishing *Tannhäuser* for breach of commercial practice by putting the ballet in the wrong place. Meyerbeer represents the mechanization of epic; in him the creative process becomes automated. His conception of his art is actually not political, as Heine's parliamentary analogy suggests, but industrial. His operas are assembled by a division of labor between himself, Scribe, the scene-painters and the singers. Each one is a fashionable variation on a formula which remains unchanged, like successive models of the same car. He is a musical tycoon. The "totality of objects" which Hegel made the criterion of epic becomes, in this commercialization of the form, simply a totality of expensive and gratuitous effects, disclosing the machine at play.

Wagner jokes that Meyerbeer had commissioned Scribe to furnish a scenic equivalent of Berlioz's orchestra. Berlioz, like Wagner himself, was mocked by cartoonists for the elephantine scope and monstrous inventiveness of his orchestration; both were treated as crazed scientific projectors. Berlioz in one comic print uses a telegraph pole as a baton. Wagner was credited in a Viennese cartoon with the invention of "Die Bayreuther Tonkunst-Dampfmaschine," a musical vapor-machine. Hanslick, describing the tinted steam and gas apparatus of Bayreuth in 1876, remarked that Wagner could not have composed the *Ring* before the invention of electric light. Wagner's imagination and that of Berlioz turn technology into art, and in the composition of their so-called epics, *Der Ring des Nibelungen* and *Les Troyens,* both approach Meyerbeer in remaking epic in the image of the mid-nineteenth century.

As Heine had attached Meyerbeer to the institutional models of democratic parliament and the army, so these works of Wagner and Berlioz resemble two other institutions characteristic of their civilization. One is the factory, in which aesthetic creation follows the logic of the industrial process by which wealth is created, and which turns works of art into assemblages of moving parts like machines. The other is the museum, a factory in which the past is organized and processed.

The epic of Berlioz is made possible by the startling superimpositions of the cultural museum. Hofmannsthal, it will be seen in a later chapter, makes the triumvirate of Homer, Shakespeare, and Rembrandt, joined in museum-like proximity, the guardian spirits of opera; similarly, Berlioz in *Les Troyens* imprints on Virgilian history the form of Shakespearean drama. The work is also a Meyerbeerian factory of effects, jumbling together marches and ballets, hunts and storms, duets, quintets and septets, harvest festivals and funeral ceremonies, like the plenitude of exhibits at an industrial fair. Wagner's epic investigates and exem-

1. A neoclassical design for *Les Troyens* in 1863 by A. Casse: the Greeks in search of the Trojan treasure, in the finale of Act II.

plifies the contradictions and stresses of the political and economic order. György Lukács calls Homer's account of Achilles' weapons epic because it not only describes what they look like but how they were made. The epic poet is one who is not yet estranged from the processes of manufacture which sustain his society. In this sense, Wagner's subject is the nature of epic: the *Ring* is about the creation of wealth and, as a result of this, the formation and dissolution of society. It applies Lukács's epic intelligence to history, reasoning backwards from the present (*Götterdämmerung*, the starting-point of the dramatic composition) to the remote past in which society is convened (*Das Rheingold*, the last of the dramas to be written, but the first for which music was composed). Shaw believed the *Ring* to be an allegory of industrial power, but it is also a late, catastrophic embodiment of the process it describes, a vast self-combusting machine, not so much a cathedral as a dynamo, one of those "symbols of ultimate energy" which, for Henry Adams, had confounded the idea of the cathedral. But it is a dynamo housed, at Bayreuth, in a temple which is also a museum.

Although *Les Troyens* and the *Ring* touch at various points, they are antithetical in form and doctrine. They face one another as epics of the two contrasted kingdoms of romantic imagination, the lyricism and lucidity of the Mediterranean and the visionary dreariness of the dark, fearful North. Nietzsche turned to *Carmen* as a respite from the intoxicating gloom of Wagner, but he might have found the same limpidity and clear, dry air in *Les Troyens* and the same finality of organization, the opposite (for him) of the polyp-like infinitude of Wagner's scores. Between them, the pair of works seem out to act out Goethe's epigram declaring the classical to be healthy, the romantic diseased. Berlioz indeed describes the establishment of the classical world-order, Wagner the degeneration of the romantic world-order.

The agent of Berlioz's eventual Roman order is Enée, entangled by the Carthaginian queen but at last persuaded to sacrifice her to the mission the gods have entrusted to him. The agent of Wagner's political order is nominally Siegfried, created fearless and untrammelled so as to extricate the gods from their prison of compromises and broken treaties, but beguiled—through his discovery of Brünnhilde—into treachery and destroyed. Historical prophecy fulfills itself in Berlioz's epic; in Wagner, all hope of change is abandoned and progress aborted by a series of brutal accidents. The literary imagination of Berlioz is historical; that of Wagner is mythic, eternally returning to where it began. *Les Troyens* therefore ends in a justification of history, a fortunate fall, atoning for the casualties of Troy and Carthage in a vision of Rome; *Götterdämmerung* ends in flood, fire, and falling masonry. The huge edifice of the tetralogy collapses, leaving behind nothing but the babbling and gurgling of the Rhinemaidens, with which it all began. As they recapture their ring, myth cancels out history. In history men strive and suffer in time, which ensures constant change and improving growth; myth reveals time and therefore history to have been cheating illusions. Because the world is perpetually, mythically, the same, the effort of history is energy wasted. The end of the *Ring* rescinds the radical optimism of the beginning; Schopenhauer casts out Bakunin. Whereas the Virgilian catastrophes of Berlioz are the midwives of history, those of Wagner are terrifying in their excessiveness and pointlessness. Like Milton parching his paradise to a desert and locking out Adam and Eve, Wagner destroys the world he has so laboriously created in taking his leave of it. The holocaust is puzzlingly gratuitous, for the return of the ring was meant to revoke the curse. Does Valhalla catch fire by accident, as accident leads the Holländer to spy on Senta and Erik and, drawing the wrong conclusions, leap to destruction? The orchestra asserts the redemptive power of love, but there is no one left for it to redeem.

In Wagner, myth confounds history and in doing so discounts and destroys his characters. Those of Berlioz, however, are sacrificed to an historical inevitability. Enée connects the two parts of *Les Troyens;* but, as Siegfried is superseded by Brünnhilde, who inherits and inverts his epic purpose and frees the gods not by political initiative but by mystical renunciation, so Enée remains dramatically subordinate to the pair of heroines, Cassandre and Didon. They occupy the center because they are the dramatic victims of history. Theirs is the private, inconsolable life of sentiment, whereas Enée forges indeflectibly on, out of the opera into history. His relation to them is like that of Daniel Deronda to Gwendolen Harleth in George Eliot's novel: Deronda departs to confront his epic destiny, leaving Gwendolen closeted in personal interests and selfish affections; he is a force, she a mere individual. Berlioz turns the Virgilian hero into a nineteenth century embodiment of the march of mind; Enée is as relentless in his exit from Carthage as the wooden horse is in its entry into Troy. Hence the work's oddly passive conception of his heroism: he is history's instrument, the "inexorable loi" Cassandre invokes. He finds, indeed founds, a world elsewhere, and Cassandre and Didon are transitory episodes in his career.

History grants Enée immunity from the drama, whereas Siegfried, created to serve history, is destroyed by entanglement in the drama. Setting out to perform new deeds of epic prowess, he blunders instead into the political guile and corporate ambition of the Gibichung hall. The boundless career of epic achievement prophesied for him contracts into the confused events and impostures of a few days. The hero is fettered by a novelistically minute time-scheme, since despite the gigantism of Wagner's operas the duration of their action is fatally brief: Siegfried forges the sword, kills the dragon, and awakens

2. Siegfried in Gotham: Lynd Ward, 1931.

Brünnhilde one day; the next day he leaves her, is drugged by Hagen, and returns to win her for Gunther; the next day she conspires to destroy him, and the day after that the revenge is accomplished.

The *Ring* compresses its epochs of mythic time into a series of painfully protracted moments. This constraining, peremptory time is a guarantee of tragedy, since it refuses the characters the chance to grow and the time to save themselves. Brünnhilde's reaction when Siegfried awakens her on the rock expresses the coincidental terror of Wagnerian time and the claustrophobia of Wagnerian space: she is, despite her elation, appalled by the neatness and inevitability of the design which has sent Siegfried unknowingly to release her from a punishment which she incurred to save his life. Wagnerian providence leaves his characters with the afflicted sense of being immured in a forbiddingly unified work of art. The years between Brünnhilde's transgression and her awakening have been elided, just as the circularity of the *Ring* and its thematic repetitiveness ensure that no time seems to have elapsed between the theft of the ring and its recovery, except the four days which the audience has spent listening to the music. And even this free time Wagner begrudges to his audience and wishes to appropriate. One of the reasons for drawing listeners to Bayreuth was to remove them from the private lives they would otherwise resume during bouts of abandonment to Wagner. The circumstances of Bayreuth made these interstices a limbo, passed in a tedious suspension, waiting for life itself to resume with the next evening's music. Wagner treats his audience as he treats his characters, who are permitted no liberty to shape events for themselves.

Wagner's imagination rushes towards destruction. Many of his operas seem destined to end happily and have to be wrenched, as if redemptively, into tragedy. Hence the misunderstanding in *Der Fliegende Holländer,* or the invention of an artificial test to separate Lohengrin and Elsa, or the quarrel over ownership of the ring, where catastrophe is precipitated by a near-farcical confusion of identities. Wagner intervenes to thrust his characters towards disaster, to save them from shaming good fortune. Like Wotan, he has a talent for destroying those he loves. The ring at times seems a device for exterminating characters while begging the questions of motive and responsibility—they simply touch it, and all is over with them. Wagner's art, like Henry James's, depends on limiting conditions, taboo-like prohibitions and a reticence which binds both the artist and his characters. The uncle must never be notified of events at Bly, the article manufactured at Woollett must never be named, Maggie must not declare her suspicions. The play of high intelligence in James, and the drive towards dissolution and redemption in Wagner, require this elaborate etiquette to separate the sainted, abnormal field of art from the demeaning contingencies of life. Isolde can never simply leave Marke, and the ship on which he is traveling to bring pardon and release must arrive too late. The possibility of domestic happiness would be as fatal to Tristan and Isolde as explicitness would be to Maggie and the Prince.

*Les Troyens* presses ahead towards a promised future. Its vision is millenial, that of the *Ring* terminal. One of the last words Brünnhilde cries out in the ecstatic duet which concludes *Siegfried* is "Götterdämmerung": she is already anticipating the holocaust, rather than trusting to a renewal of life. *Les Troyens* develops forwards, but the *Ring* was created backwards. The arch of anterior narrative was implicit in the original account of Siegfried's death, so that each subsequent stage of the drama unfolded by Wagner in reverse order serves as a further preparation for the end. The action is compelled to grow by regression, ruminatively extending back to the beginning, because in a world where the end is fated the only way forward lies in reinterpretation of the past. Wagner's own movement in the dramatic composition, reaching the beginning in successive efforts to assign responsibility for the end, is doubled by the obsessive retrospection of his characters, who hope to briefly delay the end by fretting to understand the beginning.

The optimistic extensions of Berlioz's time are equalled by the amplitude of his space. His opera comprises separate and distant places, jagged, panicky Troy, lazy, lotus-eating Carthage, and the phantasmagoria of imperial Rome. A tragedy in Troy yields to a comedy in Carthage, which as Enée arrives is celebrating seven years of prosperity. The universe of *Götterdämmerung,* in contrast with the pastoral expanses of *Siegfried,* seems oppressively small: Siegfried has no sooner set out on the Rhine than he is becalmed in the Gibichung hall, his career over. Shaw criticised *Götterdämmerung* for betraying the austerity of music-drama by inflating it into grand opera, but the magnification of size is countered by diminution in the drama. Having been declared omnipotent, the characters cannot grope and suffer through a tragedy: they can only be brought low by stagey devices, a potion, a magic helmet, a squabble about a love-token. The fearless Siegfried becomes pathetically malleable;

Brünnhilde's warrior-maid heroism declines into shrewishness, allowing Siegfried to treat her shrieks of rage on the spear as ill-bred scolding.

Though defeated and humbled in the drama, the characters are raised aloft by the music. Wagner indeed reverses Nietzsche's rule of destruction through the Dionysian potency of music and salvation through the Apollonian clarity of drama. The frail and ignorant Siegfried is laid to rest only to be resurrected and ennobled in the funeral march and in Brünnhilde's elegy. Brünnhilde herself strides into the final scene shrewishly, mocking Gutrune's grief as childish puling over spilt milk; but she goes on to revise her own motives in apologetic retrospect and to effect her own transfiguration while music submerges drama and the pyre is ignited in the orchestra. The effect is that of levitation, of absolute disjunction between the guilty worldly character and its unspoiled spiritual emanation. An arbitrary break occurs at some point in the development of Wagner's people. The drinking of the potion and, later, death effect such radical breaks in the psychological histories of Tristan and Isolde; similarly, Parsifal the dolt abruptly attains sanctity, and Kundry the inarticulate beast becomes a seductress and then a penitent. As they are jolted from a material to an ideal existence, from person to spirit, the characters acquire new identities, or else exchange identities between themselves: Siegfried declares that he and Brünnhilde are now one composite self; Tristan and Isolde solemnize a similar transfer in their duet, as he takes on her identity and she his. Such absorptions of individuals into psychic pairs mark the final stage in Wagner's dissolution of what D. H. Lawrence called the old, stable ego of character, buoyed up by an exterior world in which it has possessions and employment and ambitions, into something internal, fluid, forceful, and allotropic. The shifting states of consciousness of this new type of character are exposed not by the drama, which must make translations into rational acts and a judicious calculation of behaviour, but by the music, whose ambiguous chromaticism mixes motives and confounds responsibility. Despite the equivalence between drama and music insisted on in his theory, Wagner's people are characterized by music, not drama: the truth about the vengeful Isolde of the first act is intimated by the orchestra, with its unappeased yearnings which betray her own factitious, dramatic version of events. The consequences of this change from drama to music extend to the modern novel where, in part under Wagner's influence, people are characterized not through external action or conversation but through the silent, and hence musical, life of thought and feeling. Terence in Virginia Woolf's *The Voyage Out* wishes to write a novel about silence, recording the things people don't say. Such silences are transcribed by music: the orchestra in the first act of *Tristan und Isolde* can admit things which the characters dare not say about their relationship.

Traduced by the drama, Wagner's characters are resurrected by the music. This is a liberty the classical characters of Berlioz lack. Though sustained by a vision of the future, they cannot use it to turn their deaths into victories. Waltraute remonstrates with Brünnhilde, and all she predicts is confirmed at the end, but Brünnhilde in her intransigence appropriates the prophetic role, chooses general destruction, and argues that her access of wisdom atones for the wreckage of the world. Cassandre also predicts doom

for Troy, and no one listens, but she is not contemptuously expelled like Waltraute; she dies summoning
the women of the city to self-defensive suicide. So
different is the mental atmosphere between the two
works that Cassandre's Wagnerian ravings about a
love–death

> (La mort jalouse
> Prépare notre lit nuptial pour demain)

are dismissed as evidence of insanity, while in *Götterdämmerung* it is the wifely normality of Gutrune which
is abhorrent.

Departure and death are sources of pain and embarrassment in Berlioz. Enée, cursed by Didon, can only
fall back on yet another rallying cry of "Italie!" and
drag off in his wake soldiers who find the historical
destiny a quixotic bore and would rather stay ashore
eating venison and talking Phoenician to their Carthaginian girlfriends. Didon helplessly leaves the duty
of revenge to Hannibal, resigning herself to die in
misery. Nothing Wagner's characters do, however,
becomes them like their dying, which is scarcely a
submission to bodily necessity or a retreat from shame
but a spiritual triumph and an ultimate repudiation of
nature. Brünnhilde's immolation is an act of dazing
gratuitousness, like Tristan's tearing off his bandages
or Isolde's willing herself to expire. The classical heroines perish more bitterly, with none of the Wagnerian
rapture of erotic impatience, Cassandre calling on the
gods of Hades, Didon descending "aux enfers."

If death in Wagner is voluptuous, so the apocalypse
remakes the world in vacuous innocence and peace.
The mythic inconsequentiality of *Götterdämmerung,*
with the orchestra transporting us back to where we

began, contrasts with the ironic historical stalemate which concludes *Les Troyens,* where the survivor is not the orchestra—the elemental existence into which the characters have been absorbed—but the chorus. As Wagner is drawn back into the past, Berlioz projects himself forwards. The chorus vows eternal war on the descendants of Troy, but its anger is placated by history in Didon's reconciliatory foresight, with the Capitol hovering in the air, surrounded by a panoply of legions, poets, and artists. Berlioz acknowledges a history outside the scope of his work; the omnivorous Wagner engorges everything into that work and once it has ended, rather than permitting life to resume, directs us back to begin the work all over again.

These opposed conceptions of time correspond to the different ways the characters have of remembering. Myth makes all the past eternally present, and this condition recurs in miniature in the memories of Wagner's characters, who have the dubious blessing of total recall. Wagner lies between Wordsworth and Proust as a poet of the inexorable movement backwards and inwards, an artist for whom life is not lived forwards but relived by being remembered backwards. No event has meaning for a Wagnerian character unless it can be incorporated into his past. Hence Siegfried's long hesitation over the sleeping Brünnhilde and his much-derided invocation of his mother: the actual embrace must wait on the ingestion of this shock of erotic experience into his past. Hence too the logic of Hagen's assault on Siegfried, which is aimed fatally at his memory. The assault on his recollection of the past is followed by an attack literally from behind: Brünnhilde advises Hagen to stab Siegfried in the back because, knowing he would never turn from an enemy, she left it unprotected by spells. Siegfried even models his death, when it comes, on a recapitulation of the awakening of Brünnhilde. Musically, the work itself is equally backward-looking, turning the epic habit of deference to past grandeur, expressed usually in honorific lists and tribal genealogies, into an introverted psychological dependence on the past. The texture of motifs, perpetually reminding the characters how they have come to be what they are, is an intricate machine by which the work develops musically, as it was planned dramatically, backwards.

While in Wagner history is a nightmare from which the characters cannot escape, in Berlioz it allows for restitution and renewal. Enée, telling Didon about Andromaque, like a Victorian novelist confiding in an epilogue what his characters are up to now the novel is over, releases her from history into a private and happy future. She marries Pyrrhus:

> Elle aime son vainqueur, l'assassin de son père,
> Le fils du meurtrier de son illustre époux.

Andromaque has compromised the tragic conception of her solemnised in Troy in the clarinet-accompanied dumb show during which, in mourning with Astyanax her son, she lays flowers at the altar. Didon's sense of tragic decorum is offended, but Andromaque's progress beyond grief answers to the relaxed humanity, the Shakespearean quality of resilient nature sustained by its unheroic determination to be simply the thing it is, which Berlioz sets to complicate and weaken the hieratic severity of epic.

For although the classical subject belongs to Berlioz, he treats it romantically, whereas Wagner gives to his Gothic material the austere shape of classical drama. Berlioz's participation in the romantic disembodiment

of Shakespeare, turning him from a dramatist into a
lyrical poet and psychological novelist, will be discussed in the following chapter. In *Les Troyens* as well
he opens out Virgilian epic into demotic Shakespearean history. Here as in *Henry IV* history has a
double plot, and the tragic conscientiousness of princes
is disputed and disowned by their comically feckless
subjects. Berlioz has an unoperatic, Shakespearean
readiness to concede other points of view, however
damaging to the single-mindedness of epic. In this, his
text converges with Verdi's Shakespearean conversion
of history from political decision to social suffering,
the subject of the next chapter, and anticipates the
novelistic democratization of epic which G. K. Chesterton found in Browning's *The Ring and the Book*.
Chesterton called that poem "the great epic of the age,
because it is the expression of the belief. . . that no man
ever lived upon this earth without possessing a point of
view." It is "the epic of free speech," indulging as
Shakespeare does the uprising of comic subjects
against their tragic masters. Berlioz too confounds historical record by introducing private testimonies, the
free speech of individuals to whom history is an irrelevance and war at best an occupation. Thus before their
suicide the Trojan women sing an oddly joyful hymn,
and a Greek captain, though an enemy, is startled into
sympathy and an aesthetic wonder:

> Quoi! la lyre à la main! . . . de ce noble transport,
> J'admire malgré moi la sublime ironie!
> Cassandre! . . . qu'elle est belle ainsi chantant la mort,
> Bacchante à l'oeil azur s'enivrant d'harmonie!

Ascagne entices Didon to renounce her epic role of
widowed queen by slipping Sichée's ring from her
finger; a Phrygian soldier is homesick; portentous

voices counsel the chieftans, but to the sentries the chieftans are simply hearing things. The travail of history remains incomprehensible to those whose concern is their own physical safety, but it can also invade and scar private feelings. The logic of Enée's desertion of Didon is the same as that of Hal's rejection of Falstaff. Both are men of public destiny, "monstres de piété" as Didon says, who pass brutally through personal attachments and discard them without remorse, conquering politically at the expense of their humanity.

Romantic literary forms have an instinct for turning into their opposites, attaining freedom by self-contradiction. Thus epic for Wordsworth contracts into an account of the growth of his own mind; or drama, instead of connecting characters in active relationship, evacuates itself and dwindles into lyrical soliloquy. Berlioz and Wagner both deal in paradoxical, self-controverting form. *Les Troyens* turns Virgilian epic into its formal opposite, Shakespearean history; contrariwise, Wagner imposes on the violent anarchy of his saga narrative the classical rigor of Aeschylean tragedy. Berlioz and Wagner suggest in music the polarity romantic critics found between the negative capability and delight in disorder of Shakespeare and the egotistical sublimity of Milton, and Wagner's subjugation of his sources closely recalls Milton's labor of explication in reasoning the fables and riddles of *Genesis* into a philosophical and scientific epic. The *Ring* is the *Oresteia* of the gloomy north—a denunciation of the ways of gods to men.

In contrast with the oppressive unification of Wagner's musical structure, Berlioz's appears to be a loose aggregate like an eighteenth-century number opera. But with the romantic instinct for paradox and for making forms contradict their own rules, it includes numbers only to turn them inside out. The octet is transformed from a Meyerbeerian machine, a parliamentary debate or military drill to return to Heine's metaphors, into a troubled communal soliloquy, nervously overheard. The blithe pastoral song of Iopas is interrupted half way through, and Hylas drifts off to sleep during his song. Or else the numbers are jumbled together in the chaos of contraries Schlegel thought central to romantic art and to the colliding improprieties of Shakespeare's tragicomedy. Thus Carthage is dislocated into a series of ceremonies, entertainments, and private encounters, and the variability of scenic form means that the frame of the action is constantly altering. Carthage is in succession a model economy, its builders diagrammatically presented with a set-square and axe, its sailors with rudder and oar, and its farm laborers with a sickle; a Claudean pastoral landscape during the hunt, yet also, with its murmuring sea, a maritime society; and a militaristic epic community during the ceremony of the weapons.

While *Les Troyens* is exotically asymmetrical, Wagner's forms have a fearful symmetry, forbiddingly self-sufficient. *Tristan* is ordered with an austere equilibrium: the first act is allotted to Isolde, the third to Tristan, who there provides his interpretation of the events of Isolde's first-act narration (a technique of alternating points of view which the novel was to adopt); the middle act they share. *Götterdämmerung* has a similar incongruous neatness, the signature of an artistic temperament as rigidly exclusive as that of Berlioz is generously, even haphazardly, inclusive. Each of Wagner's enormous acts begins with prophetic agents, in the outer acts the trios of Norns and Rhinemaidens, in the shadowy center their antagonist, the phantom of Alberich appearing to Hagen (or emerging from within him, utterly unlike the ghosts pressing Enée onwards, which are the impartial voices of historical necessity). These guardians then yield to a series of patterned encounters between Siegfried and Brünn-hilde. In Act One their initial jubilant duet from the prologue is cancelled at the end by the parodic wooing in the Tarnhelm. In Act Two they converge in a trial of strength during their competitive oaths. In Act Three they are reconciled in separation, each celebra-ting an image of the other—Siegfried revives the radi-ant maiden of the awakening, Brünnhilde expunges his treachery and restores him to sun-like purity.

Berlioz described Shakespeare as a "fracas sublime," and *Les Troyens* has something of the same creative abandon, admitting and nonchalantly reconciling clas-sical heroism and Elizabethan cowardice, Trojan hys-teria and Claudean serenity, the drilled formality of grand opera and the erotic intimacy of the hymn to the night (a dreamy enchantment, not the violent oblivion of *Tristan*) or the duet in the garden by the sea. *Les Troyens* is two operas in one, as *The Winter's Tale,* which also makes the journey from a tragic court to a beneficent pastoral, is two plays in one. Both are held together by their own experimental recklessness. In contrast with this open, adventurous form, Wagner stands guard over his achievement as jealously as Hagen over the Rhine. *Götterdämmerung* might be called a sublime fracas, but in its case the phrase is not jovially chaotic but threatens disaster. As the orchestra overpowers the characters and sweeps them away in its torrent, so the creativity of *Götterdämmerung* seems pledged to destruction, of its characters and at last of itself.

If, however, this work is set in relation to the rest of the tetralogy, an organic disunity like that of Berlioz begins to appear. Philosophically, the *Ring* arches across the history of romanticism from *Das Rheingold*, conceived in terms of the revolutionary politics of 1848, trusting that the world can be altered by reform, to the disintegrativeness of *Götterdämmerung*, which with late-romantic fatalism discounts political action and withdraws into the solitary safety of mysticism. But from the literary point of view, the development is backwards, and the epic of *Götterdämmerung* is only the beginning of another arch which spans the history of literary form. Reading forwards in the order of musical composition from *Das Rheingold* in 1854 to *Götterdämmerung* in 1873–4, there is a stylistic gap after the second act of *Siegfried*, the lacuna in which *Tristan* and *Die Meistersinger* were written. Likewise, in a literary reading which follows Wagner's own backwards elaboration of the idea from *Götterdämmerung* in 1848 to *Das Rheingold* in 1852, each segment of the *Ring* represents a separate literary state. *Les Troyens* is two operas in one, the *Ring* four operas in one.

The progress back from one to the next has an evolutionary logic. *Götterdämmerung*, both the end and the beginning, is epic, because epic, while the beginning of literature, has as its subject the end—the fall of civilizations or, in Milton, of man. It deals always with the final, calamitous conflict. Beyond *Götterdämmerung*, *Siegfried* belongs to the genres of pastoral, which treats not the politician or soldier but his apprenticeship in private life, and of romance, which describes the hero's journey through the world towards self-discovery. The next part to be unfolded in Wagner's backward movement, *Die Walküre,* approximates to the form which emerges next in the evolution of literature, the novel. Its characters are no longer warriors as in epic or chivalric questers as in romance but citizens, members of a society. This opera is a series of dialogues in which errant individuals are constrained by the loyalties and contractual obligations which comprise their society. Beyond this is *Das Rheingold,* musically the beginning, as literary form the conclusion, since it has renounced the personal affections and materialistic detail of the novel and is concerned with the war of ideas. It abstracts the novel into philosophical debate, as Shaw praised Ibsen for doing, and hence, in Shaw's sense, it is less an opera than an oratorio—a conversion of oratorio from religion to economics, for it dramatizes not the operation of grace through nature but the corrosion of money in society. Characters in it do not exist passionately for themselves, as in *Die Walküre,* but as the spokesmen for policies.

As a compendium, the *Ring* contains in turn examples of the major forms through which modern literature has developed. The duality of *Les Troyens* has a similar implication: *La Prise de Troie* is tragic epic, swift and terminal; *Les Troyens à Carthage* is pastoral, indolently expansive, an interlude, for the Trojan hosts, between bouts of epic exertion. The coupling of the two parts is like a juxtaposition of the *Iliad* and the *Odyssey:* embattled epic unfurls into exploratory romance; the beleaguered stasis of the siege opens out into the episodic divagations of a self-serving individual. Berlioz has reversed the combination of the two Homeric forms in his source, the *Aeneid,* in which romance is succeeded by epic: Virgil's first six books constitute an *Odyssey,* the last six an *Iliad.*

3. Siegfried and Brünnhilde in Kensington Gardens: Arthur Rackham's design for the final scene of *Siegfried*, 1910.

Reading backwards through the *Ring*, the dynastic ambitions which make *Götterdämmerung* an epic slacken in *Siegfried* into the romance of the juvenile hero's quest for knowledge of himself. The romance's location is a pastoral landscape where the murmurs of the forest confide Siegfried's sentimental longings and its creatures act as his mentors. He learns about parenthood from the nestlings, roedeer, and foxes, conscripts the bear for his practical joke against Mime, and is warned and guided by the wood-bird. Siegfried's intimacy with nature is not an attribute of epic heroism, but belongs to the protagonist of romance, whose yearning is to know about himself and his origins, not to perform brave deeds, to recover an obscured childhood, not to confront the responsibilities of manhood. The young Siegried is what Papageno calls himself, a "Naturmensch," a feathered creature not yet separated from the community of animals, unready for human individuality. Like Papageno, this untried Siegfried is a comic hero, who undertakes his chivalric outings not in the hope of earning martial honor (though that at once becomes his object in the epic *Götterdämmerung,* when Brünnhilde sends him off to perform "neuen Taten" of prowess) but so as to understand the meaning of fear. And this, ironically, he learns not from the dragon he slays or the god he swaggers past but from the defenseless woman he kisses.

Siegfried's is a sentimental journey which begins in a practical joke and ends in an embrace. For others too the action is a game. The Wanderer confronts Mime in a competition of riddles, and his conversation with Siegfried is contorted by conceited word-play about his missing eye. Mime babbles frenetically through his music. Alberich's laugh rings out with savage glee when Siegfried strikes Mime down. Siegfried's response to the access of uncertain feeling when he cuts Brünnhilde's breastplate is the nervously joking announcement, "Das ist kein Mann!" Comedy is the natural medium of a society as close as this to the predatory guile and tricky inventiveness of the animal world. Siegfried's laughter is hearty, Mime's hysterical, Alberich's brutally sarcastic, the Wanderer's gravely superior. The dragon is a greedy dotard who expires, revealing his secrets to Siegfried, as a fawning domestic pet. The wood-bird is pert and teasing, indicating the path but flirtatiously vanishing before Siegfried can reach the mountain. Rustic, maudlin, and falsely naive, *Siegfried* condescends knowingly to the state of innocence it describes.

In *Die Walküre* the homeless ramblings of romance are confined by the form of the novel. The young Siegfried's journey ends on a bare mountain summit, the elder Siegfried's in the hall of a clan, but Siegmund's flight leads him to a single domestic interior where he is at once enmeshed in private emotional antagonisms (not, as in the Gibichung hall, in dynastic ambitions). Siegfried is a hero jauntily seeking dragons to slay and maidens to woo. Siegmund cannot afford this chivalric exuberance: he is a fugitive without possessions and therefore an affront to Hunding's proprietorial concern for his house and his wife. Hunding scorns him by pointing out that he lacks even a weapon to defend himself. To the bourgeois, property is an extension of his person, and Hunding appraises Sieglinde as a valuable chattel plundered by a gypsy. The anarchist's invasion of the bourgeois marriage is to Hunding as assault on the rights of property, and to

Fricka an impious assault on the laws of sexual propriety which she polices. Siegmund's error is to have stumbled out of his tribal wilderness into a society knit by contracts, acquisition, and the balance of power, and he falls forfeit to it. Roaming through the forest in wolf skins, Wotan and his offspring are safe in an epic world of endless feuds; but inside a society guarded by laws and prohibitions, force is unavailing because the enemy is nameless and invisible. Siegfried in his epic and romance at least knows his antagonists, but Siegmund is the novelistic, unknowing victim of interests and institutions. Fricka, whom he never sees, condemns him because the idea of his transgression offends her.

*Die Walküre* is a work of intimate dialogue or domestic dispute or whispered confession, rarely concerning more than two or three characters at a time. These characters are related subjectively—and in this sense *Die Walküre* accords with the mental, and therefore musical, definition of the novel proposed by Hofmannsthal, which will be discussed in the fourth chapter. Brünnhilde, for instance, is as she tells Wotan not an independent agent but a patient externalization of his will, a surrogate doing what he wishes but dares not openly perform. She, Siegmund, and Sieglinde are indeed Wotan's fantasies, psychological instruments by which he hopes to move the world while appearing to remain himself unmoved. He experiences Siegmund's fight with Hunding as a phantasmagoria in which his will strives against his duty, just as Sieglinde experiences it as a delirious nightmare, and the final scene with Brünnhilde is a quarrel between his political calculation and his emotional conscience. Confession or revindication are private and cloistered in *Die Wal-*

*küre,* whereas in the epic of *Götterdämmerung* all revelations are made scandalously public before the vassals. Considered as a novel, this stage in the development of the *Ring* is a psychological study of a Wotan who is brooding and immobile, no longer the artful tactician of *Das Rheingold* and not yet the unoccupied traveller of *Siegfried* for whom the world's mysteries have been cheapened into quiz questions.

*Das Rheingold* progresses beyond the human emotion which, once Brünnhilde is infected with it by Siegmund, is the source of the novelistic complication of *Die Walküre.* In form it suggests Ibsenite drama, which chastened the liveliness and chaotic plenitude of the nineteenth-century novel, replacing characters with creatures who are the delegates of ideas, replacing action with an exposition of the material and spiritual fates which inexorably connect these ideas. Shaw insisted on its derivation from *Die Zauberflöte,* and the connection between them will be analysed in the chapter devoted to Mozart's opera. Both works are classified by Shaw as oratorio rather than opera. Sacred oratorio discloses the workings of grace in nature, and *Das Rheingold,* secularizing the form, is a diagram of a worshipful plutocracy and of the magic attractions of wealth and power which make economic society work. It contains no human beings. In it, the prophecy of Shaw's She Ancient in *Back to Methuselah* has been realized: "The day will come when there will be no more people, only thought." Those who participate in it have no existence beyond their coveting of the gold. The Rhinemaidens enjoy the gold in aesthetic innocence, rather than corrupting it into a means of power. The dwarfs mine it, amassing wealth in industrious anonymity. The giants construct with it. The leisured

gods, sleeping in their fields, need it to maintain a political system which reserves to them the profits from the
toil of others. Like the plays of Ibsen and Shaw, this is a
drama of ideas dialectically energized in discussion,
not of characters in action.

The *Ring* is often wrongly called an epic: that term
applies to only one of its instalments, for the tetralogy
extends from epic, the drama of force, through the
comic apprenticeship of the epic hero in romance, to a
novelistic study of the evasive and guilt-ridden society
which looks to the hero for its redemption, and finally
reaches in the prologue the most modern of its forms,
the abstract, ideological morality play. Wagner called
it music-drama, but that term is more a slogan than a
literary definition, and the conditions of the work's
reversed and introverted development frustrate drama's impulse to advance, to happen. It is closer to the
novel's examination of private conscience than to
drama; and this enmity between the two, intensified
by music which transcribes novelistic affection and
subjective complicity rather than the active externality
of drama, is pursued in the chapter which follows.
That chapter concerns Shakespeare. In Berlioz, Shakespearean history, truculently comic and unruly, confounds the severity of classical epic; Wagner too envis-
aged his operatic form as a union between classical
tragedy and Shakespeare, between the ritual theodicy
of the one and the self-interrogatory soliloquies of the
other. Both turn Shakespeare into a romantic, which
means converting him from a dramatist into a musical
novelist.

# 2. Operatic Shakespeare

The romantics appropriate Shakespeare by denying that he is a dramatist, and the peculiar metamorphosis to which they subject him has consequences for musical form. As this chapter will demonstrate, the plays are treated either as lyrical monologues, in which case the corresponding form is the symphonic poem, or else as frustrated novels, which is the implication of Verdi's use of them. The alternative musical forms are related: the symphonic poem is a species of musical novel, since in its submergence of plot in atmosphere it snubs the drama and prefers to record, like the novel, the meditative life of motive and self-examination.

The symphonic poem hopes to do Shakespeare the service of saving him from this extrovert, activist form of drama, which the romantics could only believe was forced on him by financial convenience. It answers to the needs of his characters: Hamlet longs to escape from the busy routine of revenge drama into the inactive privacy of the dramatic monologue; Macbeth is traduced by the drama, which presents him as a murderous fiend, whereas in the solitude of his lyrical meditations he reveals a lucid, entranced detachment from the crimes the drama alleges he commits. The symphonic poem satisfies the yearning of these characters to exchange the compromises of dramatic action for solitary pensiveness.

From Charles Lamb's dismissal of performances of

Shakespeare as shoddy attempts to shackle a dream in material form, to Hofmannsthal's argument that the plays come to life inside their solitary reader, not on a crowded stage, romantic critical tradition insists on separating the introverted music of Shakespeare's poetry from the dramatic coercion of his plots. Hofmannsthal in particular characterizes Shakespeare as a musical novelist. The actor's role has been usurped by the reader, who like an Aeolian harp makes himself an instrument on which the score of an individual play performs itself. The reader, Hofmannsthal says, carries *The Tempest* in his pocket. The text has been reduced to a pocket score, and what Shakespeare wrote is vivified not by an actor's declamations but by the reader's permitting it to live in him. Thus the characters of any play do not belong to the strutting and fretting stage, but make up the fractious community of the reader's selves—reading *The Tempest* we make of ourselves the vacant island where there is space for Prospero's magnificence as well as caves of boyhood fears for Caliban to lurk in. In Shakespeare, Hofmannsthal says, the music alone matters; and this music expresses itself not through the mechanism of dramatic action but by way of a discipline of self-contemplation closer to the novel. The virtue of the symphonic poem is that it prevents the characters from singing and makes them think about themselves instead.

For Arthur Symons, attacking the fussy externality of English acting in the 1890's, "the rhythm of Shakespeare's art is not fundamentally different from that of Beethoven"; he classifies *Hamlet* as a symphony and *Romeo and Juliet* as a suite. This suggests a justification of Berlioz's apparently perverse *Roméo et Juliette,* a hybrid of symphonic poem and opera, which allows everyone to sing except the hero and heroine. The chorus is omnipresent; a contralto (a beatified Nurse, perhaps) praises love and identifies it with poetry, whose supreme secret Shakespeare understood and took with him to heaven; Mercutio celebrates Mab; and the Friar transforms the burial into a reconciliatory cantata. But Romeo and Juliet are silent—because they are spirits, haunting the atmosphere. When they talk, they do so instrumentally, not vocally. In the love scene Juliet chatters nervously on the oboe, while the violas murmur calmingly on Romeo's behalf. At its periphery the work approaches opera, because the history of the lovers has public implications which the contralto and bass proclaim, and Mercutio has a noisy vocal ebullience which cannot be suppressed. But at the center it is symphonic because the privacy of love demands reticent musical paraphrase, not verbal eavesdropping. Although Berlioz called his hybrid a dramatic symphony, the two forms are at odds in it, and symphony absorbs drama.

The correspondence between the dramatic monologue, the form in which the romantic Hamlet takes refuge from the exigencies of action, and the symphonic poem is made clear in *Lélio,* the monodrama Berlioz attached to the *Symphonie fantastique* in 1832. Here the protagonist of the symphony returns to life after the dream of his execution to lament his misery and at last console himself in directing a performance of his fantasy on *The Tempest.* Symphony is first turned into drama, as the various movements of the *Fantastique* are made to stand for episodes in the life of an artist. Then, in the series of songs which echo Lélio's depression or act out his fantasies of violent reprisal, drama is re-translated into music.

Lélio himself passes in the course of the work from the tutelage of Hamlet to that of Prospero: that is, from a dramatic monologuist wresting his grief into words to a composer imperiously commanding the elements and his own emotions in art. Lélio blames Hamlet for his mood of paralyzed dread and, remembering the ghost on the battlements, hears music around and within himself as an ideal orchestra plays for a chorus of shades. The monodrama is performed in Hamlet's "mental space"—Hofmannsthal remarked of the mental performance of Shakespeare, "There is so much space within us." Once the monodrama is translated into music, the orchestra too becomes an image of mind, and it is therefore hidden behind a curtain.

Having indulged his self-pitying moods, Lélio eventually determines to conquer his irresolution and his melancholy illusions. In doing so he changes from Hamlet into Prospero, sitting down earnestly to work on an Italian cantata derived from *The Tempest*. Prospero controls his play by a magic which is in fact rigorous artistic technique: he is a cold, autocratic artificer, with absolute power over the characters who enact his fantasies for him. Lélio is therefore changed from a helpless poet into an irritable conductor, since Prospero writes the masque which is the action of *The Tempest* as well as directing its single, definitive performance. Accordingly the Prospero of Berlioz tyrannizes his players into perfection of ensemble, reproves the singers for holding their scores in front of their faces, maneuvres the chorus like a general distributing his troops, and bestows grudging praise at the end. Hamlet overheard music which was playing inside himself; Prospero wills the fantasy into external form. Hence, when he takes over, the curtain which had screened Hamlet's mental orchestra rises to disclose Prospero's ranked performers ready to play the finale. But when Lélio dismisses his musicians and is left alone on the forestage, the curtain closes off the domain of his power, which was after all only an extension of fantasy. He hears the obsessive theme from the symphony again, and relapses into the suffering passivity of Hamlet.

Romantic criticism made Shakespearean opera virtually impossible because, instead of procuring an alliance between music and drama, it made enemies of them. The Hamlet and Prospero of Berlioz are musicians who despise the idea of participation in a drama. As Hamlet, Lélio longs for the repose of death and is sure that continued life means only augmented suffering. As Prospero, he composes a drama which others, under his impassive academic direction, perform. In this musical appropriation of Shakespeare, his words are expunged along with his characters and paraphrased symphonically, as in *Roméo et Juliette;* or else the drama is slighted, as in Berlioz's setting of *Much Ado* as *Béatrice et Bénédict,* in which the plot attaching to Hero and Claudio is excluded to make way for the antics of the pedantic musician Somarone, who performs an "épithalame grotesque" and discourses on fugue. Music invades the drama, but it is too capricious to assume the responsibility of controlling its development, so that the crucial scene of Benedick's eavesdropping on the conversation about Beatrice's love for him is left in speech.

Since words are considered, in this romantic theory, to be a makeshift medium of exchange only, a convention of the surface remote from the musical spirit or atmosphere of the play, they can be removed from their position in the drama and put to other uses in music. In this way Berlioz is able to commandeer the duet of Lorenzo and Jessica from *The Merchant of Venice* for Enée and Didon in *Les Troyens*. In the play the series of legendary fancies about moonlit nights discovers ironic disparities between the separate worlds of mercenary, prosaic Venice and fabled Belmont, the seat of justice and musical concord. Lorenzo and Jessica are refugees from Venice, ill at ease in the enchanted language of Belmont, and although their compliments begin in mythology with Troilus, Thisbe, Dido, and Medea, the artifice lets them down into their own, comfortably imperfect world, and they begin to make half-joking and half-guilty accusations—Jessica unthriftily steals from the wealthy Jew, enticed by false vows, and shrewishly slanders her love. But while Shakespeare's characters cheapen mythology, dealing out its stale exempla like playing cards, Berlioz takes the same passage and startlingly vivifies it. His hero and heroine walk into the museum of legendary hearsay whose contents Lorenzo and Jessica are absently reviewing. The statues begin to move. Enée and Didon casually treat the gods as peers and acquaintances: she refers to "votre mère Vénus" following Anchises to the groves of Ida, and accuses him of a coldness unbecoming in the son of Cytherea; as they leave, Mercury materializes to recall Enée to his mission. It is Didon's fate to join the catalogue of fair, forsaken women, and although Berlioz tactfully omits the lines, Lorenzo has already noticed her as such:

In such a night
Stood Dido with a willow in her hand
Upon the wild sea-banks, and waft her love
To come again to Carthage.

Reckless infidelity to the letter of the plays is, romantically, a way of serving their spirit. They long to be lyrical novels, and Berlioz's disruptions help to grant their wish by undoing them as drama. Though careless about the letter, Berlioz was possessed by the spirit of Shakespeare. So, in a quite different way, was Verdi. They divide him between them: Berlioz re-creates something of the Shakespearean form, while Verdi is genuinely Shakespearean in feeling.

For Berlioz, Shakespeare is the kind of artist Schiller called sentimental: ironic, self-interrogating, delighting in irregular forms and quizzical, conceited verbal wit. Berlioz's own unstable structures—the lopsided partnership of terse tragedy and expansive pastoral in *Les Troyens,* the use of festive comedy to proclaim the rights of genius against the state in *Benvenuto Cellini*—match Shakespeare's heteroclite collisions of tragedy and comedy. His instrumental virtuosity transfers Shakespeare's verbal exuberance to the orchestra, in the writing for the horns in the scherzo of Queen Mab, for instance.

For Verdi, Shakespeare is the kind of artist Schiller called naive: self-effacing, a force of calm and natural order rather than disruptive, self-exhibiting intelligence. Whereas Berlioz becomes impatient with Shakespeare's characters and, as in *Béatrice et Bénédict,* dismisses them in order to write musical journalism against his enemies, Verdi, like Shakespeare himself, rests in astonished contemplation of characters whose mysterious objectivity he respects. For him, consequently, the secret of character lies as much in words as in music. Hence the potency of Lady Macbeth's entrance reading, rather than singing, her husband's letter. Though a convention in contemporary opera, here the reading of the letter implies that Lady Macbeth remains a dramatic character, resisting complete translation into opera. Verdi drew attention to the distinction in demanding for the part a voice which was harsh and devilish, a voice, as he said, virtually incapable of singing. While in Berlioz music obliterates drama, Verdi insists that musical values remain properly deferential to dramatic values: during the rehearsals for *Macbeth,* he urged the protagonists to concentrate on declamation of the text, not mellifluous phrasing.

Both Berlioz and Verdi implicitly accept Hugo's account of Shakespeare as an artist dealing in romantic contradictions of extremes, a Christian realist in whose double plots the sublime and the grotesque, the tragic aspirations of the mind and the comic confinement of the body, are yoked together. But they make characteristically different uses of the perception.

Berlioz understands it formally, Verdi emotionally. In Berlioz the juxtaposition of tragic and comic, of spirituality and coarseness, Hamlet and Falstaff, occurs less within single characters than outside them in his abrupt, indecorous dramatic structures. Shakespearean tragicomedy is a property of form. In *La Damnation de Faust,* for instance, the intellectual ardor of the philosopher clashes with the bestiality of the tavern, the rapture of his vision of Marguerite with the prurient alarm of the neighbors, as Marguerite's lonely expectancy is accompanied by the lecherous songs of prowling students. Tragedy and comedy are happening simultaneously, in different parts of the structure.

But in Verdi the same contrariety is a property of character. Hugo's Triboulet, the hunchbacked jester in *Le roi s'amuse,* is a character in whom sublimity of sentiment redeems physical grotesquerie. Paternal love sanctifies his deformity, just as in Hugo's Lucrèce Borgia (Donizetti's Lucrezia) maternal care purifies the moral ugliness of the murderess. Verdi, turning Triboulet into Rigoletto, preserves the Shakespearean ambivalence. As a dramatic character Rigoletto is gross and debased, but as a musical character he is exonerated by his selfless concern for Gilda. The same complexity recurs in Verdi's Falstaff. The drama declares him a braggart, a glutton, and a treacherous intriguer; music, however, confers on him a grandiloquence of imagination and a lyrical enthusiasm which, despite his ugly obesity, make him a figure of comic wisdom and spiritual grace. Music pardons all faults, and Verdi employs it with Shakespearean generosity, allowing characters condemned by the drama to save themselves by singing. Much is forgiven Marguerite in Dumas's *La Dame aux camélias* because she has loved greatly; all is forgiven Violetta in *La Traviata* because she has sung beautifully. Music grants her a way of revealing her goodness in seraphic singing which is denied to her literary prototype.

For Berlioz Shakespeare appeared in a thunderclap of chaotic inspiration, as a baleful visionary. Lélio blames the terrifying profundities of *Hamlet* and the dolorous lyricism of Thomas Moore for the revolution which has disrupted his being. Shakespeare is a ghostly visitant, a disturbing god. Lélio addresses him as an obscure demon: he passed through earthly life without belonging in it (just as his plays suffer themselves to be represented on the stage, without belonging there), and is therefore as mysterious and untraceable as those other poets whose genius seemed to the romantics to disappear into divinity, Homer and Ossian. Verdi's reverence for Shakespeare has none of this troubled sublimity. He regarded the plays with affectionate familiarity as a literary scripture and by his bedside at Sant' Agata had two Italian translations of the complete works.

Shakespeare is for Berlioz an anguished lyrical poet whose soliloquies can be borrowed as oblique personal confessions: Berlioz assumes the role of Hamlet, or casts himself as a world-renouncing tragic victim by quoting Macbeth's "Life's but a walking shadow" at the outset of his memoirs. Shakespeare is for Verdi a craftsmanlike novelist who modestly departs from his creations, never using them, as Berlioz does, for self-dramatization. Shakespeare preserves a wondering distance from his characters, and Verdi has a similar forbearance. As Shakespeare, in Keats's phrase, comprises and comprehends both Iago and Imogen, so Verdi distributes music with compassionate impartiality between opposite points of view—the patriotic zeal of Amonasro and the emotional fidelity of Aida, the noble indignation of Anckarstrøm and the vagrant, impulsive affection of his wife. His novelistic understanding of Shakespeare means that Verdi's drama is historical, and while in Berlioz history impersonalizes, making of the Virgilian hero an abstract idea of historical inevitability, in Verdi history is the incorporation of private emotion in a community.

Politics in Berlioz mercilessly cancels bonds of affection; but in Verdi politics grows out of primary affections, and it is this tribal duty which makes Aida's choice so painful. She complains that her fatherland has cost her dearly, but it is her father who has demanded the sacrifice: the two ideas, "patria" and "padre," are the same.

Patriotism is a political magnification of parental authority, and many of Verdi's most moving dramatic situations describe the choice daughters must make between sexual love and filial devotion, which means loyalty doubly to father and fatherland. Berlioz's Enée is a hero from neoclassical drama confronted by the symmetrically simple clash between passion and duty, Venus and Mars; the heroines of Verdi are more tormented and helpless creatures, compelled to choose between two kinds of love which should support one another. As Verdi personalizes history, every allegiance implies an emotional commitment and every institution becomes a repository of emotional trust. Public destinies are the same as private interests because both are directed by the affections. Germont defends social morality on behalf of a daughter he must protect. Posa's friendship for Carlos is synonymous with his conversion of him to the cause of Flemish liberation. When Gabriele Adorno discovers that his enemy Boccanegra is Amelia's father, he promptly changes political sides and joins Boccanegra against the patricians. Because personal affection can so readily be converted into political conviction, Verdi's first audiences found punning superimpositions of the two in the unlikeliest places. Elvira's longing for Ernani to release her from the repellent embrace of Silva was cheered as a cry for liberation from the Austrian oppressors: the action became a crudely allegorized cartoon of political protest.

It is through the politics of Italian unification that Verdi assimilates Shakespeare and remakes his drama as a nineteenth-century novel. The subject, constantly alluded to with cautious obliqueness, knits Verdi's operas together into a vast episodic historical study, just as the Wars of the Roses and the problems of succession make a sequence of Shakespeare's history plays, despite the chronological disorder of composition. Criticism has rearranged the history plays into two tetralogies, the first arching across the reign of Henry VI to the accession of Richard III, the second returning to treat the deposition of Richard II and the reigns of Henry IV and Henry V. In the same way, history equalizes Verdi's operas, abolishing differences in time and space to make them a composite statement about the fate of Italy. The oppressed Jews of *Nabucco* and the refugees from Macbeth on the border are the same people; Simon Boccanegra makes propaganda for Italian unity in imploring his fourteenth-century Genoese councillors to make peace with Venice in the name of Wagner's hero, Rienzi; in the eighteenth century Alvaro and Carlo in *La Forza del Destino* adopt pseudonyms and travel with the Spanish contingent to Italy to fight the Germans; like a recurring character in Balzac, Charles V is elected Emperor in *Ernani* and returns in the guise of a friar to rescue Don Carlos from the inquisition; Attila wrests Italy from papal control.

As has been argued in the preceding chapter, the casual links between Wagner's operas—Lohengrin's acknowledgement of Parsifal as his father, the projected meeting between Parsifal and Tristan—give them the cyclical shape of chivalric romance. But the political action which connects Verdi's most disparate operas resembles Shakespearean historical drama made over into a nineteenth-century novel.

To the nineteenth-century understanding, Shakespeare's pair of tetralogies had democratized history; beside a political interpretation of events, which explains history through the wilful acts of individual rulers, the plays record the obscure, nameless, unremembered doings of non-political society, and find here a principle of continuity which survives the personal catastrophes of rulers. Social history and its conservative inertia take over from political history as the *Henry IV* plays proceed: in Eastcheap or Gloucestershire, life continues, listlessly indifferent to the shifts of political power. Falstaff leads this rebellion of society against politics, and he makes it a rebellion of comedy against tragedy. Political history is necessarily tragic because each ruler dies miserably conscious of error and the infections of power; social history is comic because resilient, unselfconscious, and endless.

This historical vision is adopted by the nineteenth-century novel, in Balzac's ambition to take as his subject "the four or five thousand persons which a society offers," and in Tolstoy's epilogue to *War and Peace*, which asks the Shakespearean question, how can the history of a nation be written? Balzac answers the question biologically. Society is an historical organism, and the novelist is required to be a natural scientist, patiently investigating the habits and environment of the creatures he studies. Tolstoy answers it philosophically. His conclusion is, however, the same. He defines power as the collective will of all the people, which they invest for convenience in rulers: hence the purpose of historical argument is not to account for the decisions of the leaders, who are deputies of the people, but to fathom the original motives of the nation. "The movement of nations," Tolstoy suggests, "is caused not by power, nor by intellectual activity, nor even by a combination of the two, as historians have supposed, but by the activity of *all* the people who participate in the event."

In the same way, Verdi's operas assume that history is not a record of individual initiatives but of the flux of humanity and peoples. Decentralizing history, they reveal it, in Babylon, medieval Genoa, or eighteenth-century Velletri, to be a mass impulse, and like Shakespeare's plays they document the irritations and amusements of those whose lives are anonymous and remote from the positions of command. In company with the pusillanimous sailors or grumbling sentries of *Les Troyens,* whose derivation from Shakespeare was noted in the first chapter, the homesick recruits, camp-following shopkeepers, gypsy recruiting agents and curmudgeonly monks in *La Forza del Destino* are members of a vast migrant natural community which exists beneath the attention of historical memorial. Their omnipresence, oscillating between Spain and Italy, is an image of the tidal movement of masses described by Tolstoy. Like the Shakespeare of *Henry V,* as the nineteenth century interpreted that play's patriotism, Verdi makes himself the dramatist of national self-consciousness, though that consciousness is articulated not by a militaristic individual like Henry V but by the national community. Individuals place a vain trust in action; the community patiently waits and suffers, and Verdi's finest choruses—"Va pensiero" from *Nabucco,* "Patria oppressa" from *Macbeth,* the phoenix chorus led by Foresto in *Attila*—make of its passivity a force of moral conviction and wise forbearance.

Even a tragic hero like Otello emerges, in Verdi's introduction of him, from the crowd, and speaks on its behalf. The first scene of *Otello* is Verdi's most imaginative dramatization of a crowd, because it catches the elemental impersonality of its feelings. The Cypriots and soldiers, alternately anxious and uproarious, first raging against the storms and sandbanks, then delirious with joy when victory is announced, are the voice of the tempest. The mob is itself an element, unstable, excitable and imperious. From the confused violence of its emotion Otello's voice separates itself, in his cry of "Esultate!" and then subsides, as if overwhelmed. As if undifferentiated from the elements, Otello does not take sole credit for the victory over the arrogant Moslem but thanks the hurricane for its assistance. The hurricane is the convulsive crowd at the quayside, and its outbursts do not so much describe as enact the battle.

The elements of howling wind and heaving water then give way to another, fire. After Otello's disappearance into the fortress, the crowd—literally, a force of nature—is characterized by the bonfire it lights, capricious and treacherous. As the stormily martial elements of air and water had assumed human form in the apparition of Otello, so now the ingenious, destructive element of fire materializes in Iago, whose temptation of Cassio insinuates itself in flickering vocal interjections, like tongues of ironic flame, as the chorus celebrating the fire dies into silence. Otello's announcement of victory had given vocal expression to the titanic trumpets which the chorus described blaring in the sky. Now Iago's vicious chatter and the blazing enthusiasm of his drinking song ignite the crowd. The fire of rejoicing turns into a deranging heat: the world throbs, Iago says, when drink lights him up. As the fire chorus had kindled, flared, and then thinned into dimness, so the scuffle explodes in cries of revolt and satanic possession and, when Otello reappears, retreats as inexplicably as fire. *Otello* reincorporates the unruly community into nature, and turns the political crowd which passively resists tyranny in the earlier operas into a rioting mob. The crowd does not return after the first scene—Lodovico is greeted by the decorous court, not by the Cypriot populace—perhaps because its ferocity and cruel impulsiveness have been absorbed into the nature of Otello.

The submergence of political in social history gives a peculiar significance to Verdi's final Shakespearean hero, Falstaff. During the reign of Henry IV he conducts a subversive campaign against the heroic notion of history as a succession of valiant deeds, but he possesses an inverse, paradoxical heroism of his own which connects him with the truculent populism of Verdi's earlier operas. The cowardly indestructibility which enables Falstaff at Shrewsbury to turn even death into an occasion for sham and play-acting is comically justified because it is self-protective: Falstaff devotes himself to keeping alive his vital spark, rather than squandering it with the reckless folly of Hotspur. His contempt for martial honor is not abject and envious like that of Parolles in *All's Well That Ends Well,* and it derives from a reasoned and mockingly dignified philosophy. To Falstaff, the integrity of his body is as sacred as integrity of mind is to Hamlet, and the better part of valor lies in the discreet preservation of that body, which is the seat of comfort and delight. According to his own logic, Falstaff is more valiant than the reptilian Prince John or the dangerously volatile Hotspur. He has an exuberant self-satisfaction which is boastfully heroic in comparison with the crafty reserve of the former; and whereas the latter risks and destroys himself in histrionic excess, Falstaff wins a victory by keeping himself alive. Though sourly condemned as unpatriotic, Falstaff has made a kingdom for himself in the corpulent acreage of his flesh, and he rouses it to brave deeds with infusions of sack. His body is a commonwealth, and he its jovial monarch.

The elation of Verdi's Falstaff may seem distant from the despondency of Berlioz's Hamlet, but the apparently opposite aspects of Shakespeare with which the two composers sympathize are secretly similar. Both characters, for different reasons, shun participation in drama. Falstaff's swelling self-possession is the body's equivalent to Hamlet's vigilant independence of mind. Both dream of the same state of peace, released from the requirements of dramatic action. Hamlet believes he might attain this quietus by silencing the querulous mind and punishing the greedy body; Falstaff does achieve it by over-indulging the body and allowing it to inundate the mind. Hamlet detests the activism of revenge as Falstaff does the exertions of military prowess. Both aspire to that dreamy passivity—for Hamlet, death, for Falstaff, an indolent satiety—which romantic critics understood as a state of lyrical privacy and self-sufficiency incompatible with drama. Neither has any desire to act, so that in the plays they retire into the safety of the monologue. They wish to luxuriate in their sense of themselves, to enjoy the pleasures of stupor—and music, being as Kierkegaard calls it the medium of sensuous immediacy, allows them to do precisely this.

Thus the translation of Falstaff to music confirms and enforces the Shakespearean character's dual opposition to politics (which connects him with Verdi's approximation to the novel of social history) and to drama (which connects him with the dramatic monologue and its correlative, the symphonic poem, written for him by Elgar). Boïto's libretto, which chooses not the subversive Falstaff of *Henry IV* but the suburban adulterer of *The Merry Wives of Windsor,* may seem to contradict this, but it does not. In the first place, Boïto's text imports the most significant of Falstaff's passages from the political play, his creed of ideal apathy and cautionary self-preservation; and secondly, its particular brilliance lies in its fusion of the two Falstaffs, who are separate in Shakespeare's management of the character and in critical commentary on him. Marrying the political and the sexual Falstaffs, Verdi and Boïto make a summary statement about the character more complete and, in its discovery of his romantic meaning, more complicated than Shakespeare's.

Shakespeare's relations with his characters are mysteriously oblique, often tolerant and forgiving, but at times fickle and even careless, and it may be that, having permitted Falstaff to stretch the *Henry IV* plays out of shape and to appropriate the second part as a series of occasions for self-dramatization, Shakespeare turns against him. He is not an artist who generally exploits characters by recalling them for sequels, and Falstaff's reappearances progressively diminish him. Already in the second part of *Henry IV* he is distempered; after his rejection he dies in senile delirium in *Henry V*. That death occurs offstage, which is the final snub: as Auden pointed out, Falstaff has already shammed death once onstage and cannot be given the chance to flaunt his immortality a second time. Death must happen elsewhere, and be reported by reliable witnesses. But Falstaff was resurrected by royal command when the queen, as legend has it, demanded a play about Sir John in love; and it seems suspiciously as if, irritated or bored by the commission, Shakespeare transferred the blame to Falstaff. Exhumed, he is a sadly reduced creature, unable to sustain his heroic effrontery, worn down to the indignities of concealment in dirty linen, fouling in a ditch, and travesty, when he masquerades as the fat woman of Brainford to escape from Ford.

The sovereign Falstaff who was witty in himself and a cause of wit in others is now the victim of the wit of others. His merry persecutors speak of him not with the worshipful solicitude of Doll Tearsheet at Eastcheap but with feminist revulsion. Mistress Page vows revenge "as sure as his guts are made of puddings," Mistress Ford calls him a "gross wat'ry pumpion" or a whale melted by fiery lust in its own grease. The comedy is shaming and sullying, marking down Falstaff as a beast. He assumes the guise of the fattest rutting stag in the forest, and dreams of the erotic metamorphoses of the gods, but in his case the shape-changes are ugly and demeaning. He is first made an ass and then, Ford adds, an ox too. In the narrow, intrigue-ridden and vindictively proper society of Windsor, populated by small people (Slender says Anne Page "speaks small like a woman"), Falstaff's heroic pretensions make him lumberingly and vulnerably outsize. He is a whale, belly bloated with oil, thrown ashore by a storm incongruously in Windsor, or a Mount Pelion requiring giantesses for mistresses. Mental nimbleness can no longer save him. His body betrays him, pierced like Hamlet's by slings and arrows.

*The Merry Wives of Windsor* ought to be Falstaff's monument but disappointingly is not, perhaps because Shakespeare had tired of the character. Falstaff is in the *Henry IV* plays only to controvert their political and military dogma. His successes there are occasional and joking, but he is bound to be censured and cast out. Hal warns him of this from the first, so that the comic creativity by which Falstaff distends and extends the plays is merely a desperate stratagem to delay his inevitable expulsion. He does not belong in *Henry IV: The Merry Wives* ought to release him into pastoral privacy, unmolested by duty and responsibility, but Shakespeare treats him instead with dismissive curtness and sets the wives to hound and degrade him. This scourging of Falstaff suits some interpreters. Fuseli's various pictures of the torments he is subjected to by the wives, malign ballerinas with fetishistic coiffures, make Falstaff a neurotic victim from Fuseli's own private world of sexual fantasy and fear. But generally it has been softened. Vaughan Williams's opera *Sir John in Love,* for instance, ignores the callousness and disgust and makes Windsor a place of folksy rural innocence.

Boïto and Verdi do not sentimentalize *The Merry Wives* in this way: they redeem it. Music not only returns Falstaff, as Boïto said, to his "clear Tuscan source" in Boccaccio, but regenerates the spoiled Shakespearean character, allowing him to become what, in the play, he can only pretend to be. Wearily lying about his age, Shakespeare's Falstaff is engaged in a hopeless battle against time and its retributions. But Verdi's Falstaff, singing "Quand'ero paggio," makes himself juvenile, lean and sprightly by the way he sings, thinning a bulky voice to an agile wisp. The musical Falstaff is saved from the deliquescence of the flesh, since opera employs the body—the singer plays upon an instrument concealed inside himself—but makes it an emanation of the spirit. Hamlet in the guise of Lélio heard an orchestra playing morosely inside his head; Falstaff's body turns into an uproarious orchestra which does not murmur internally but externalizes itself in a jovial cacophony. Recovering from his dunking at the Garter, Verdi's Falstaff adapts his prototype's speech from *Henry IV* about the bellicose properties of sherris and describes his intoxication musically. Wine, he says, awakens a trillsmith in the reeling brain, who makes the heart pound and conveys his excitement to the world outside, which trills sympathetically in musical abandon:

> . . . e il giocondo globo squilibra una demenza
> Trillante! E il trillo invade il mondo!!!

Opera alters the balance of power between Falstaff and his persecutors, enlisting on his behalf its own form of heroism, which consists in setting a solitary individual to sing against and dominate the mass of an ensemble. Violetta or Desdemona do so in their disgrace, at Flora's party or during the reception of Lodovico's embassy, and vocal heroism is their defense against their accusers. Falstaff sings in bold, assertive soliloquy; the wives chatter together in meticulous ensemble. His merriment is audaciously individual; theirs is a concerted mockery. His body, the reverent object which he salutes in "Va, vecchio

John" or begs the wives to spare at Herne's oak, with-
stands the siege of a united community, and this gives
new point to the military recollections from *Henry IV*.
The operatic Falstaff considers himself an extrava-
gantly valiant Hotspur, too generous a figure for the
reduced, civilian world into which he has been demobilized, and Ford addresses him rousingly as a man
of war and a man of the world. His brave deeds are
performed in daring isolation, whereas his opponents
hunt in safe packs. Even his lust is blamelessly gratuitous, disinterested because mercenary.

The social position of the shabby, superannuated
Falstaff of *The Merry Wives* is correspondingly altered.
In *Henry IV* Falstaff bluffingly acts the part of the king
in the tavern. The opera grants him his wish and makes
him a monarch, whose flesh is his kingdom and whose
obesity is a mode of imperialism: "Questo è il mio
regno. Lo ingrandirò." His cronies at the tavern constitute a court. Installed at the Garter, he behaves with
royal disregard for the property of others, beating Dr.
Caius's servants, violating his house, and wearing out
his bay mare, but receiving ambassadors like Quickly
or bringers of tribute like Ford with lordly condescen-
sion. His court, feckless, strife-ridden, and intemper-
ate, is set against the domestic economy of a suburban
household, where Alice supervises the collection of the
laundry and fusses over the living-room appoint-
ments, nervously adjusting the chair, the lute, and the
screen in preparation for her titled guest.

The regal and the bourgeois are differentiated musically. Falstaff's idiom is heroic, that of the wives lyrical: the disparity is the same as that between the
trumpet-toned martial urgency of Otello and the
plangent entreaties of Desdemona. Both sides are res-
cued from Shakespeare's brisk, diminishing epi-

grams. Falstaff begins mock-heroically, but persever-
ance and his energetic determination to survive earn
him at last a genuine comic heroism; the wives begin
mock-lyrically, parodying the flourishes of the dupli-
cate love-letters, but seem to acquire a lyrical fondness
for their quarry, in Alice's final rapt, floating quotation
of "Ma il viso mio su lui risplenderà," which catches
for a moment the tone of Desdemona, and in their
echoing calls through the dusk near the inn.

As Berlioz had turned the versatile, comically adept,
and glibly witty Hamlet of Shakespeare into a morose
romantic poet making art from his diseases, so music,
in rescuing Falstaff from Shakespeare, discovers for
him a quite unexpected romantic significance—and
one which avows his kinship with the nineteenth-
century Hamlet. Music subjects Falstaff to disorient-
ing translations in time and space like those which
Wilde's Salomé, the subject of the final chapter, experiences. As Boïto acknowledged, the English knight
becomes a sybaritic Tuscan. Even more oddly, just as
Wagner removes Tristan from the formalities of
chivalric romance to make him a neurasthenically
self-divided hero of the late nineteenth century, so
Falstaff ceases to be a Vice from the medieval interludes or an Elizabethan braggart and becomes, like
Tristan, a romantic decadent.

The connection between Falstaff and Tristan is implicitly made by the actress Eleanora Duse, at the time
Boïto's mistress, in a letter of 1895. She had recently
read *Trionfo della Morte* by d'Annunzio, her next lover,
a novel which describes a besotted pair who suicidally
act out the calamity of Tristan and Isolde. Their erotic
avidity demands more than the appeasement of appetite and can only be satisfied by embracing its apparent
opposite, the "pure ideality" and abstractness of death.

The operatic Falstaff, from Duse's point of view, is their natural contemporary. He too feeds and irrigates the flesh in order to silence it and predicts his own extinction in the scene outside the Garter. Duse objects to both Falstaff and the Tristan of d'Annunzio as traducers of vital energy, creatures who have subsided into will-less satiety. Her letter begins by scorning *Falstaff* as "sad stuff," and goes on to attack d'Annunzio for maligning "every great *test* of courage—every heroic effort *to put up with life*—all the great agonizing sacrifice which is *to live.*" The irascible logic of her argument is closer to agreement with her decadent enemies than she realizes: she concurs with them in calling it a sacrifice to remain alive, and in assuming that death—into which Falstaff sees himself helplessly declining, into which d'Annunzio's enfevered lovers hurl themselves—is the object of instinct and desire. But she concludes by dismissing the opera and the novel together: "neither *Falstaff* nor d'Annunzio." She has translated the Elizabethan toper into the period of wine, roses, and the systematic derangement of the senses.

A similar transposition proves to be dramatically ruinous in *Otello,* however. Making Iago a romantic satanist, as Boïto does by equipping him with a sardonic Credo, unbalances the Shakespearean action by filling in the envious, motiveless, prosaic vacancy of the character. Otello's natural medium is music, but Shakespeare's Iago cannot exist in it, because, not knowing what he is, distrusting and ironically disowning all his emotions, a shifty and self-detesting negator, he has nothing to sing about. Offered the opportunity for demonic triumph after the death of Desdemona, he refuses even to speak.

Equally, the tender lyricism of Verdi's Desdemona smudges the prosaic, anti-musical qualities which make the Shakespearean character so touching and so vulnerably different from Othello, and suppresses her uneasy and inadequate translation of herself from the wondering auditor at his recital of his campaigns to his intrusively anxious domestic companion, insisting on accompanying him into military service and fussily entreating him to wear his gloves or eat nourishing dishes. With characteristic practicality she responds to Othello's Tristanesque wish to die in bliss at the moment of reunion with her in Cyprus by touching wood and hoping for a placid connubial future. Even in her panic she makes a desperate appeal to practicality and propriety as Othello attacks her, begging him to kill her tomorrow but let her live tonight. The pity of their relationship is that love does not vouchsafe knowledge of one another: he treats her as an acolyte ministering to his idea of himself, but she treats him as a spouse to be coddled and cajoled, whose military splendor makes him even more boyishly susceptible to feminine management. In the play they die miserably divided, and Othello knows that fiends will snatch his soul at compt. But the opera joins them in the erotic after-life of *Tristan:* as Otello dies on a kiss, the orchestra consolingly murmurs the music of the initial love-duet. The tragic wit of the play, necessarily blunted by the opera, lies in the forced relationship between the musically grandiloquent Othello and two characters dangerously unlike him, immune to his musical exaltation: an uneloquent ancient who retreats at the end into hurtful silence, and a prosily solicitous wife preoccupied with domestic linen.

Whereas in the narrow, disputed space of the Shake-

spearean play these incompatible, uncomprehending
people are yoked in intimacy, the opera compresses
Iago and Desdamona into extensions of Otello. Insidiously dapper, flame-like, as was suggested in the discussion of the first act, Iago acquires the seductive musical skill exhibited in "Era la notte" and turns into a
distorted likeness of the heroic Otello, courageously
atheistic in the Credo and jeeringly triumphant when
Otello collapses after the departure of Lodovico. He
has lost that motiveless independence from Othello
which, in the play, is his most puzzling and subtle
quality. Desdemona also becomes Otello's obliging
accessory: the love-duet is created, significantly, by
assigning to her some passages of what, in the play, is
Othello's monologue of self-justification. Her crime is
to grow away from her devotional center, Otello, in-
dignantly rejecting his insult and assuming musical
control of the ensemble in Lodovico's presence. But
she renounces this independence in the final scene and
acquiesces in her impending death by singing the
willow song. The opera changes drama into something like dramatic monologue, since it removes the
play's restrictions on Othello's all-consuming
egotism.

Music does the same, as has already been described,
for Falstaff, but whereas in that case Shakespeare is
improved, even redeemed, in *Otello* Shakespeare is
slightly diminished. In granting Falstaff's wish for
hegemony, music turns him from the victim of satire
into a wise and generous comic potentate. But in
tragedy music has a different effect. The romantics in
any case tended to reduce tragedy to self-pity. The
tragic character is buffeted and destroyed by other
people; the romantic monologuist knows no other

people, but imagines that his solitude, which he complains about but jealously defends, constitutes a tragic condition. Shakespeare's Othello, whom modern critics have accused of intoxication with his own musical idiom and of specious self-vindication in his final monologue, is already close to this romantic state; opera confirms him in it.

Perhaps romantic music and tragedy are incompatible, because melody is always consoling and uplifting, and the final bars of *Otello,* like the end of *Tristan,* transmute possible tragedy into divine comedy. The symphonic poem—the *Hamlet* of Liszt or that of Tchaikovsky, the *Macbeth* of Strauss—not only romantically releases Shakespeare's characters from drama, but releases them from tragedy, because the symphonic poem is their justification. Alone with themselves, separated from the consequences of their actions or (in Hamlet's case) their inaction, they are exculpated and set free to morbidly enjoy their private universe of precious pain. The fate of Shakespeare in the romantic period, as this chapter has presented it, offers a further demonstration of the enmity between music and drama. Music's ambition is to render drama obsolete: hence the reduction of Shakespeare's complicated dramatic amplitude to the lyrical monologue of the symphonic poem. Eventually, as music extends its boundaries and requires all the other arts to aspire to its condition, opera is discounted. Ernest Newman will be found in the last chapter of this book nominating the tone-poem of Strauss as the logical successor to Wagnerian opera, which is declared imperfect because it still contains a residue of the tedious activism and dull substantiality of drama.

# 3. Operatic Allegory

In Shakespeare's case, drama surrenders to music, which claims to grant Hamlet's wish in dismissing the trappings and suits of verbal representation to probe the inarticulate life of feeling. This chapter will explore some cases in which the interchange between music and drama proceeds in the opposite direction—cases in which the integrity of a text is preserved from music in successive revisions or continuations. The two texts to be discussed, *Die Zauberflöte* and *Die Frau ohne Schatten,* are allegories, which makes them initially suspicious of music. They are intriguingly connected across the length of the romantic period, and their relationship illustrates this book's larger argument about the antagonism between drama and the novel, because in each case the revisions are designed to force a change from one form to the other. Mozart's opera seemed to the romantics to waste sublime music on a trivial and garbled text, which Goethe accordingly revises into an allegory, replacing the theatrical antics of Schikaneder with an interior exploration of mystery which defies stage representation; Auden then transports the characters into a leisurely novelistic after-life. Hofmannsthal, who in *Die Frau ohne Schatten* was making his own version of *Die Zauberflöte,* having first prepared the work as a drama and witnessed its inundation by Strauss's gaudy and violent music, rescues it from both drama and music by rewriting it as a novel.

Between the works, entangled with both, lies Gothe's *Faust,* central to an understanding of both because of its own vexed relations with music. The various recensions to be treated in this chapter all assume that the texts of *Die Zauberflöte* and *Die Frau ohne Schatten* require protection from music, which squanders their secrets and coarsens their meanings; and *Faust* is the original case of a text for which adequate music can never be composed, because the text is already music. It is an opera without music, and its integrity as an allegory depends on its keeping music at bay.

In a conversation with Goethe early in 1829, Eckermann confided that he still hoped adequate music would be supplied for *Faust.* Goethe replied that it was impossible, because the passages of terror and repulsion were not in the style of the time. The music, he said, should have been like that of *Don Giovanni,* demonic and thrusting—"Mozart should have composed for *Faust.*"

No romantic opera did justice to *Faust.* Gounod makes the philosophical quester languishing and love-sick and turns Mephistopheles into a moustache-twirling dandy with a plume in his cap. With equal irrelevance, Berlioz makes Faust a nature-poet, striding on precipices and surveying torrents. Although Schumann, unlike Gounod or Berlioz, attempted a setting of the final scene of Part II, he mistreats the mood, and the strife of experimental intellect settles into a cosy celebration of the domestic verities. The eternal woman turns out after all to be Clara, pointing sanctimoniously upwards like David Copperfield's Agnes. Liszt and Mahler reassimilate the work to symphony, which can suggest its immaterial action

and infinite space. *Faust* rejects the operatic form because it is already an opera—not a verbal opera like the
lyrically inane *Importance of Being Earnest,* but a scientific opera in which the elements acquire voices and
nature begins to sing. The laboratory tests and conjur-
ing tricks and aquatic pageants and sabbaths of the
second part are indeed a libretto, for which music was
never composed because the words themselves constitute music.

*Faust* does, however, have consequences for operatic
form. As it becomes allegorical science fiction, its hybrid lyrical and philosophical drama turns into
Wagner's art-work of the future, itself a concept of
critical science fiction. Wagner thought there were two
ways open to modern poetry, "either a complete re-
moval into the field of abstraction, a sheer combining
of mental concepts and portrayal of the world by expounding the logical laws of thought, and this office it
fulfills as philosophy, or an inner blending with music,
with that music whose inner faculty has been disclosed
to us by the symphony of Haydn, of Mozart, and of
Beethoven."

*Faust* moves in both of Wagner's directions at once,
as does, in its fourth act, Shelley's *Prometheus Unbound,*
another drama which defies the stage and abstracts
itself into music. Both poems transform drama into
the rarified conceptual universe of philosophy and science, which is Wagner's first prescription (the Pro-
methean fire is electricity, "not earthly" as Ione won-
deringly says to Panthea). Moreover, they render
drama lyrical, making nature sing: they are symphonies of science. Goethe has his mystical geology, oce-
anic triumphs, and spermatoid daemon, Shelley his
phosphorescences, meteors, and implicated orbits of

the stars performing in an elemental masque as De-morgorgon unchains all the powers of nature. In its dissolution of the substantial world Shelley's poem suggests as well those canvases of Turner illustrating Goethe's theories of color, at once apocalyptic and in-ductive, religious drama and technical treatise.

Music, Schopenhauer said, can express everything except substance. The unearthly lyrical and scientific drama of Goethe and Shelley had created the art-work of the future in advance of Wagner, who represents indeed a regression, shackling music to substance again. Nietzsche was depressed by the *Ring* at Bay-reuth in 1876 because its compromise with scenic re-alism diminished it. The horses, the bear, and the dragon anchored it to the pretences of fable, hindering its liberation into music. Romain Rolland remained convinced that Wagner was better heard in concert ex-tracts than in the theater. The invention of the invis-ible orchestra should have led, as Wagner's half-rueful joke admitted, to the invention of the invisible theater.

Romantic music works generally to render texts in-visible, to submerge them in tone-poetry. Liszt trans-lates Faust into arching, imperious themes and Gretchen into musical ideas of tenderness and simplic-ity developed by the oboe and the viola; Mephis-topheles he makes an agent who deforms and subverts the positive musical signatures of his victims. The text has disappeared into the markings of the score. But there is a case, closely connected with the anti-operatic *Faust,* of an operatic text's survival, independent of music. This is Goethe's continuation of *Die Zauber-flöte,* writen in 1795, which remained unfinished and without a composer.

These two facts—that it is incomplete, and that it

has outgrown music—answer to one another, for in
rescuing Mozart's subject from the neat finality of
Schikaneder's libretto and reopening all the questions,
Goethe's continuation is also progressing beyond opera. Unfinished, the sequel is an image of possibility.
Its fragmentariness is Faustian, because it is a provisional extension of Mozart's action, reaching sugges-
tively ahead but too impatient to grasp the enigma it
senses and therefore breaking off in honest inconclu-
siveness. Goethe allegorizes the opera, and thus introduces a change. As it stands, *Die Zauberflöte* is a puzzle;
Goethe makes it a mystery. Cryptic interpreters of *Die
Zauberflöte* assume it to be written in code and have
used masonic misogyny or Egyptian religion as keys
to that code. But an allegory is not a work in which
meanings can be produced by finding the right switch.
Rather, it is a work in which meanings emerge hesi-
tantly and ambiguously in the process of reading,
which is itself a process of initiation. The reader follows a course similar to Tamino's, battling with com-
plexities, made to choose between contradictory signs,
at every side importuned and warned off. Interpretation is a technique which can be acquired only after
trial and misadventure. Tamino's problems are indeed
those of the reader of an allegory: he knows who Sarastro and the Queen of the Night are, but what do they
stand for?

Allegory often deals with induction, as in the perils
of fire and water which Tamino and Pamina must confront, because it is an inductive form. Allegory often
deals in generation, as in Goethe's account of the offspring of the Mozartean characters, because it is a
generative form, in which significance grows with
biological gradualness, and because in it physical and

intellectual conception are made analogies of one another. This notion links Goethe's continuation of *Die Zauberflöte* with Hofmannsthal's attempt to equal it in *Die Frau ohne Schatten,* also concerned with conception and progeny. Allegory brings itself to birth: it mimes both a natural process and the ritual literary adventure of unriddling dark conceits.

However, music cannot easily cope with the prevarications of allegory or with the self-insemination which makes the reading of allegory mime the discovery of meaning by the characters inside it. The deceptions and intriguing complications of allegory belong to verbal speech alone. They are almost a disease of language, which, as Auden put it in an address at the Salzburg Festival in 1968, differs from music and painting in its lack of the indicative mood. It is only in words that we can tell lies, and this pervasive uncertainty means that "all verbal statements are ultimately in the Subjunctive." Music cannot afford the halting reflectiveness of poetry. Instead of stopping to think, Auden says, it must go on to become. Its genius is that of immediacy, so that the musical character is one, as Kierkegaard says of Don Giovanni, who lives by extempory enthusiasm, seizing the opportunity each moment presents, desperate to escape from the deathly forces of reflection. Elvira begs him to remember his past. The Commendatore warns him to attend to the retributive future. But Giovanni continues to live recklessly, and musically, in the present.

The allegorical character has none of this appetite for the immediate. He chooses to await disclosures. He is not a force of activity and exertion but the expression of a potentiality. But whereas a character in a novel would be responsible for working out that potentiality on his own, a character in an allegory is expectantly passive, knowing he can only be changed by orders and exercises, incomprehensible to him, prescribed by his mentors. Goethe's Wilhelm Meister is a composite of both types. His patron saint is Hamlet, who refuses the lure of dramatic action and insists on his novelistic right of meditation. But more than this he is Goethe's version of Tamino, patiently undergoing an initiation into the mysteries of metaphysics in the Hall of the Past, humbly accepting an idea of his own character and destiny proposed by others.

Opera which allegorically celebrates moral qualities tends to turn into cantata, as *Die Zauberflöte* briefly does, in musical recollection of Mozart's Masonic cantatas, after the Queen's rebellion is put down. Appropriately, the exequies of Mignon in *Wilhelm Meister* are celebrated in a cantata performed by invisible choirs, while four boys dressed in azure and silver fan the sarcophagus with fronds of ostrich feathers. The boys wish to remain with the dead Mignon but are won back to life by the urging of the chorus. Later four youths lift the coffin and declare that Mignon remains frozen in undecaying marble, an image of holy earnestness which her mourners may take back into life with them, "for earnestness alone makes life eternity." At these words the unseen chorus joins in, as in *Die Zauberflöte* the chorus from within completes the Speaker's instruction of Tamino.

Shaw, who distrusted the latent frivolity and aimless hedonism of the operatic form and praised Wagner as an austere musical dramatist betrayed only occasionally into the sensual excesses of opera, contrived to praise *Die Zauberflöte* for this approximation to cantata or to oratorio, and the terms in which he does so suggest an unexpected series of metamorphoses for Mozart's opera as it extends itself down the length of the nineteenth century. Although Shaw mocked the chaste scriptural monotony of English oratorio, his own musical ideal might be called oratorio intellectualized, its profanity cleansed, stiffened by the responsibilities of mind.

Oratorio does not entice its auditors into a drowsy sensuous numbness but calls them to strict moral attention. The audience may even be required to get to its feet, as during the "Hallelujah" chorus from the *Messiah*—a convention which transforms art into a duty and a pious observance. Shaw's own plays mimic the form: if *The Importance of Being Earnest* is verbal opera, *Man and Superman* is verbal oratorio. Commending *Die Zauberflöte* for its "priggish ecstasy," he sees it as leading beyond the operatic form in two directions, into symphonic intellectual debate, and into Wagner's reform of opera in *Das Rheingold*. Both tendencies contribute to the deconsecration of music, which ceases to make propaganda for religious creeds but is converted instead to participation in the evolutionary adventure of the march of mind. "Mozart," Shaw wrote in *The World* on April 13, 1889, "struck the modern secular humanitarian note in the Magic Flute, and Beethoven took it up in his setting of Schiller's Ode to Joy." In a piece published on November 12, 1890 he connected the two works in their possession of "a discomforting consciousness of virtue, and uphill effort of aspiration." The opera is no longer Masonic, nor the symphony Dionysian. Both are Comtean, and formally they merge to make an oratorio.

Mozart's transvaluation of pantomime into en-

lightened moral fable leads in turn to the *Ring,* which
also, as Shaw sees it, redeems its barbarous sources,
and frames from them an allegorical indictment of industrial power. Shaw considers the *Ring* an oratorio
which degenerates into opera when, at the awakening
of Brünnhilde, its allegorical severity and consistency
weaken. In the romantic view, the finest segment of
the *Ring* must be *Götterdämmerung,* because it is about
the suicide of romanticism; but Shaw thought it a fee-
bly conventional anti-climax. In the rationalist view,
the finest segment must be *Das Rheingold,* spare, argumentative, ironic, and didactic, and it is this work
which Shaw prefers and nominates as the successor to
*Die Zauberflöte.*

   Both *Die Zauberflöte* and *Das Rheingold* are, for
Shaw, prosaic despite their magic, employing gim-
crack marvels but abstinently exposing them as symbols of a moral condition. "Das Rheingold," Shaw
wrote in a review of June 29, 1892, "is either a profound allegory or a puerile fairy tale." By implication,
the interpreter's task, in expounding its allegory, is to
rescue it from its own puerility, as Goethe's continuation does, and as Shaw in *Man and Superman* rescues
Don Giovanni, both from his promiscuity and from
the supernatural morality which condemns him, by
endowing him with a redemptive political cause. It is
with some relief that Shaw in a further article, dated
December 9, 1891, reports that the serene law of
generalization which operates in the final scene of
*Fidelio* has rid both *Die Zauberflöte* and *Das Rheingold* of
characters, novelistic individuals with private lives and
retrogressive emotions which refuse to be enlisted for
a cause, and replaced them with dramatic figures who

are deputies faithfully representing ideas. Both works, he says, contain "personified abstractions instead of individualized characters as *dramatis personae.*"

In the lucid Hegelian universe of Shaw's drama and criticism, the noblest act is sacrifice of oneself to an idea. Individuals long for abstraction, for release from the narrowness of personal identity and the idiosyncracy of character into the instructive generality of symbol. *Das Rheingold,* containing gods, dwarfs, giants, and mermaids, but no human beings, grants them their wish. But, to Shaw's dismay, the *Ring* as it develops takes back what it has granted. The first human being to stumble into its ideological universe upsets its precarious order of abstraction: Siegmund disarms Brünnhilde when she forewarns him of his death, choosing to remain loyal to the wretched Sieglinde and dismissing the offer of immortal glory. The contagion of human emotion provokes Brünnhilde to contradict Wotan's inhuman political arrangement and costs her her godhead. Her loss of divinity equals, in Shaw's reading of it, the *Ring*'s loss of abstraction. Brünnhilde awakes as a woman in *Siegfried* and can thenceforward experience only human emotions —love, spiteful rage, anguished regret—which necessarily call on the operatic conventions *Das Rheingold* banished, so that she sings a love duet, a vengeance trio which might have come (Shaw says) from *Un Ballo in Maschera,* and mounts a pyre which did come from *Norma.* As Shaw's sympathy is with the allegorical eminence of mind, he regards the humanization of Brünnhilde as a betrayal, and he watches the progress of *Götterdämmerung* with something of the despairing detachment of Wotan as Waltraute describes him,

4. Beardsley's Alberich of 1896: a gross, furry fruit with the face of Oscar Wilde.

sitting in silent gloom on his throne clutching the splinters of his spear, destroyed by Brünnhilde's rebellion against the allegory.

His quarrel with the conclusion of the *Ring* is implicitly a quarrel with music, an attack on its seductiveness and its blithe indifference to morality and meaning. Although in a *World* essay of May 2, 1894 he defended Mozart against Ruskin, who had berated *Don Giovanni* and *Die Zauberflöte* for their heathenism, the terms of that defense suggest a covert agreement

5. Maxfield Parrish's Alberich of 1898: a Shavian miner.

with Ruskin. Shaw quotes Ruskin's declaration that true music must derive from "a lofty passion for a right cause" and points out that music is, on the contrary, fickle and untrustworthy in its versatility: "Music will express any emotion, base or lofty. She is absolutely unmoral," and depicts "Falstaff's carnal gloating over a cup of sack" as readily as the athletic humanitarianism of Beethoven's Ninth Symphony, or vulgarizes Orpheus for Offenbach as readily as ennobling him for Gluck. Although the promiscuity of music, its slippery aptitude for becoming, is urged against Ruskin, in Shaw's own aesthetics it remains a dubious and dangerous quality, because if music cannot discriminate between its potential subjects it is an enemy of mind.

Thus in allegorizing *Die Zauberflöte* Shaw is saving it not only from the trivial improvizations of Schikaneder but from the temptations of music, just as in the infernal conversation from *Man and Superman* he remakes *Don Giovanni,* transforming a hectic, agitated, sensuous opera into a sober, reflective oratorio. For Shaw, the orchestra ought to be not only invisible, as Wagner specified, but also inaudible (though brief quotations from *Don Giovanni* are permitted) because the destiny of the art-work of the future is now to outgrow music. In Wagner's interpretation of Beethoven, words are bound to be subordinate in the alliance with music; in Shaw's interpretation of Wagner, words are emancipated from music altogether, because music is mired in the regressive life of unconsciousness which words colonize and render intelligible.

*Fidelio* is for Shaw the junction between Mozart and Wagner, and it too resolves opera into cantata or allegorical oratorio. Like *Die Zauberflöte,* it is concerned with trials, suffering, and rescue, and it too consumes the operatic conventions it employs. It begins as a prosaic *Singpsiel,* in which the characters fret about money and are burdened by domestic chores (Jaquino roused from his wooing by the knocking, Leonore carrying the chains). But its form is generalized and allegorized when Leonore understands the symbolic force of her mission—she swears to free the prisoner whether he is her husband or not—and when the trumpet of judgment sounds from above to award her victory. The form then broadens further into a choral symphony, as individual lives are absorbed into a community of rejoicing. The insertion of the third *Leonore* overture between the dungeon scene and the unshackling of Florestan is often criticized for retarding the drama by making a prolix recapitulation, but in this view of the work its purpose is precisely to retard and supersede drama, to clarify the transition from operatic drama to symphonic cantata, from the conflict of particular individuals to the generalization of that conflict which is proclaimed in the sermon of Don Fernando the minister. The interlude reviews the action and, in retrospect, makes an allegory of it: recapitulation works to absorb and suppress personal crises, so that when Leonore and Florestan reappear among the chorus in the final scene they have receded into a single case exemplifying a universal law. The fraternal unity which Fernando proclaims necessarily overpasses individuals. Florestan becomes a type of man preserving his religious faith even during the severest ordeal, Leonore the loyal and steadfast wife who devotes herself to saving her husband. Pizarro is disposed of with summary absent-mindedness, he too having receded into a mere image of the tyrant shamed by avenging justice.

Goethe's continuation of *Die Zauberflöte* is a similar act of generalization. The fairy tale of the opera does not reflect on its marvels, seeing no need to distinguish between the transforming magic of the trials and self-serving magical stunts like Papageno's trick of playing his bells to make Monostatos and his crew dance.

Goethe makes it reflective. In the opera, the Queen and
Sarastro are inexplicable bogies who can artlessly
change sides in the ideological dispute: the Queen is at
first the pitiful, forsaken mother and only later is
branded a demon by hearsay; Sarastro kidnaps Pamina
to save her from this malign parent but turns her over
to his lubricious follower Monostatos. Goethe makes
them consistent representatives of opposed values.

The fairy tale facilely assumes its conclusion to be
final. Goethe implicitly challenges this by giving his
fragment a title in the genitive, *Der Zauberflöte zweiter
Teil,* indicating that his addition is a growth on
Mozart, denying the opera the last word. The Queen
returns to spoil the happiness about which the opera
was complacent. Sarastro removes himself voluntarily
from the esoteric isolation of the cult of Isis and undertakes to wander the world offering assistance to the
troubled. He is now an itinerant sage rather than the
ceremonious high priest of Schikaneder, and he encourages Tamino and Pamina to go off in search of the
infant the Queen has ravished from them and imprisoned in a gold coffin in the depths of the earth.

Goethe's fable takes over the initiatic action of the
opera but supplies it with a new purpose. Tamino and
Pamina are no longer an ingenuous pair of lovers entranced by mirror-images but parents rescuing their
offspring. In *Die Zauberflöte,* the events are a muddle
even to them: doctrinally the work is so confused that
they mutely accept the change of allegiance on which
Sarastro belatedly insists. *Der Zauberflöte* is, however,
an allegory, with a destination they can understand and
long for. The marvels of the opera diminish their own
initiative, and as they are variously pursued and en-
treated by snakes, Moors, priests, and seductive ladies,

the ordeals need not seem, to them, anything more than scenic stunts. In Goethe's continuation they are roused to defence of their child, and their progress from immobile self-pity to a generous love which risks itself in action places them in the company of Orpheus braving the underworld or Leonore venturing into the deepest of the dungeons to release her husband. Opera concerns itself generally with profane love; in the cases of Orpheus or Leonore, and in Goethe's extension of *Die Zauberflöte,* it is made to comprehend sacred love, conjugal or parental.

The rationalization extends to the subplot and reforms Papageno. In the opera, Papageno jovially intrudes on the sufferings of his betters, obstinately refuses to be changed by events, and at the last mocks the trials of fire and water by staging his own death, after imploring the spectators to intervene with applause (as Tinker Bell asks in the pantomime) if they believe in him. This is the clown at the end of his tether, garnering applause by bribes and threats.

Goethe in the first place reorganizes Papageno's relations with his superiors. He and Papagena travel from their rustic hut to the palace in the hope of comforting Tamino and Pamina, and instead of acting as the visiting card which defines his chirpy insensitivity, as it does in the opera, Papageno's music acquires an Orphic power of consolation. Tamino's anguish is relieved whenever he hears it.

Secondly, Goethe alters Papageno's relations with Papagena. In the babbling enthusiasm of their duet in the opera, they enumerate the children they expect will arrive automatically and call it the highest joy to have many, many Papagenos. Kierkegaard despised their polyphiloprogenitiveness. In his hierarchy of the erotic, Cherubino represents desire as dream, Papageno desire as search, and Don Giovanni desire as enjoyment. Papageno has not attained self-consciousness, for he seeks, Kierkegaard says, only what he can desire, and without even knowing that he desires it. Once that desire is obtained, he does not, like Don Giovanni, graduate to another more challenging object of desire, but forgets desire in the satisfactions of performance, endlessly repeated. This is what he promises Papagena, rather like Chaucer's cock feathering his consort twenty times before morning. In the pervasive sexual atmosphere of Mozart's operas, all variations of the instinct are investigated—the universal appetite and liberality of Don Giovanni, the repressive lust of the Count in *Figaro,* the exploratory titillation of *Così fan tutte,* the conjugal trust of Tamino and Pamina. But Papageno is the only character who mentions reproduction. It was one of the tasteless solecisms of Peter Ustinov's *Don Giovanni* at the Edinburgh Festival in 1973 to equip Elvira with a baby, presumably fathered by Don Giovanni: for Don Giovanni to have offspring is as impossible as it is for Tristan and Isolde to marry. But for Papageno it is the sovereign and natural impulse. As he will grow and change no further, the only future possible for him is one in which he will reproduce miniature replicas of himself.

Here lies the ironic point of Goethe's sequel, for he denies children to Papageno. He and Papagena are discovered in their woodland dwelling lamenting that the children have not arrived. An invisible choir advises them that their progeny will be born from ostrich eggs they are to find in their hut. Children do not come by clockwork: the parents have to earn them.

Tamino and Pamina search for the child Genius they have lost, but when it is released, being an essence of spirit and immaterial, it cannot rejoin its parents and vanishes again as the fragment breaks off. Here Mozart is beginning to take on the likeness of *Faust*. Because the love of Tamino and Pamina is, for Goethe's allegory, an encounter of intelligences, its product is as fugitive and demonic as the Homunculus manufactured to analyze the hero's malady in Part II of *Faust*. Wagner in his laboratory declares that the ancient method of procreation has become obsolete, and that physical congress will in future be restricted to the beasts, while man can count on a more scientifically hygienic origin. The manikin Wagner concocts is more knowing and ingratiating that the Genius who salutes Tamino and Pamina, but they are alike in representing generation intellectualized (and that, as has been argued, is both the subject and the literary method of allegory): self-perpetuation is achieved through the association of ideas, not the collision of bodies.

Hence the Genius is not corporeal and cannot belong exclusively to Tamino and Pamina. Like the clairvoyant Homunculus who yearns for a physical embodiment which he can attain only after his spiritual obligation to Faust has been fulfilled, the Genius must elude its pursuers at the end, slipping out of reach as the guards grasp at it, because ideas are migratory, provisional, constantly becoming rather than comfortably being. Papageno and Papagena do not aspire to the condition of ideas, but they too must be trained in abstention from unscientific copulatory techniques: once they are inducted into the allegory, their babies are made for them, not in test tubes but in ostrich eggs.

6. Michael Powolny's Papageno of 1918–20: a ceramic cherub from Viennese art nouveau.

7. Marc Chagall's Papageno of 1967: a bird-man of shreds and patches.

These dual procreative difficulties are the link with the double plot of Hofmannsthal's version of *Die Zauberflöte, Die Frau ohne Schatten,* which derives rather from Goethe's allegorical continuation than from Mozart.

Hofmannsthal's imperial couple cannot breed because their glassy substance lacks the warmth of flesh. Their love is unfruitful because selfishly devoted to sensual enjoyment, ignorant of any purpose beyond momentary delight. They make love every night, the Nurse reports, but each partner is worshipping a fantasy of the other, like Tamino with the portrait of Pamina, feasting upon each other with an unemotional, aesthetic greed. The Empress has acquired human shape by accident, in the course of a series of magic metamorphoses, and she yearns still for the elemental world from which she is estranged. She dreams indeed of turning into a feathered Papagena, of taking on the light body of a bird, as she tells the Nurse in her first scene. The Emperor and Empress are the hero and heroine of a fable, proudly remote from the coarseness of humanity: the Nurse is disgusted by the swarming and screeching chaos of the human world, and to the Emperor his wife is fatally sullied when, at the falcon-house, she appears surrounded by the dust and fumes of that world.

Hofmannsthal's other couple, Barak and his wife, cannot breed for different reasons, because they belong to a different literary realm. They derive not from fairy tale but from a novel, and Strauss at one stage in his preparations for the opera intended to indicate the metaphysical gap between the two couples by using a chamber orchestra for the supernatural beings and an expanded orchestra for noisy, complicated humanity.

The infertility of the Emperor and Empress is legendary, a matter of totem and taboo, since its explanation
is the curse on the talisman. That of Barak and his wife
is psychological, a matter of instinct misdirected by
emotion, and its explanation is to be diagnosed from
the reactions of the patients, not emblematically un-
riddled. They are a Papageno and Papagena bemused
by ambiguous emotion, having grown beyond the
blithe, careless state of Mozart's creatures. Barak's
generosity, providing "Speise für dreizehn," has
paradoxically cut him off from his wife, who resents
the undiscriminating distribution of his goodness (he
even takes pity on the ass which bears his skins to
market) as a snub to her. She is a woman with a ca-
pacity for love but no talent for affection. Small gestures of kindness and solicitude seem a humiliation to
her, and her inability to perform them self-
tormentingly sours her feeling for her husband. She
becomes a shrew because she cannot forgive him for
his shaming victory over her in winning her love. She
belongs hardly even to the novel, but to life indis-
creetly observed: Hofmannsthal uneasily warned
Strauss that she was to be understood on the model of
the composer's own wife, the termagant Pauline de
Ahna.

The Mozartean double plot becomes, as Hofmannsthal adapts it, almost an image of schizophre-
nia, dividing the work against itself. Myth confronts
psychology in *Die Frau ohne Schatten,* and neither
seems to understand the other. But an identity between the two apparently contradictory tiers of the
plot was established by the researches of Freud and
Jung, for they discerned that the origins of myth lie in
psychological anxieties and prohibitions. The inter-

mediary between these two literary conditions, mythic enigma and psychological explication, is allegory, which traces the lineaments of myth in individual psychological conflicts.

One strand of possibility links Goethe's Tamino and Pamina with Hofmannsthal; another, more proximate, implicates them in *Faust.* Having extricated them from opera, Goethe translates Tamino and Pamina into his own opera without music, the second part of *Faust,* where they recur as Faust and Helena, whose union is a fusion of opposites such as Schlegel found to be the energy of romantic art. In that union the modern spirit (costumed, however, medievally: Faust appears to Helena in chivalric dress; the romantic aspirant reassumes the form of the wandering knight, the hero of romance described in the first chapter of this book), questioning, agitated, power-seeking, captures the serene ideality of classical culture. From the marriage is born the spirit of modern poetry, the suicidally energetic Euphorion, who is Goethe's sketch of Byron. The elusiveness of Genius in *Der Zauberflöte* can be explained on the analogy of the antics of Euphorion, who leaps beyond the control of his parents, hurls himself into the sky, and falls from it dead. At once the corporeal part of him vanishes, and his aureole is removed to the heavens while his shade sinks into the depths, where Genius dwells, and from where he cries out, like one of Hofmannsthal's frying fishes in *Die Frau ohne Schatten,* imploring his mother not to leave him alone in the dark.

Goethe makes the action of *Die Zauberflöte* dialectical, and this entails moving the offspring of Tamino and Pamina into the center. In the opera they reach a terminus, with nothing left to experience. Goethe unsettles this domestic fixity by giving them a child who is the fusion of their separate selves, the idea they have created between them but which immediately out-grows them and flees into inaccessibility. They are re-dundant from the moment this third being, the syn-thesis, is conceived. Though they hasten protectively after him—Tamino and Pamina seeking him in the depths, Faust and Helena begging him not to yield to reckless impulses—they can neither hold him nor save him. As an idea, he must discard material form.

The unattainable synthesis represented by Euphor-ion performs a double duty in the allegory of *Faust,* as a cartoon of Byron's disastrous emotional urgency and his crusade to liberate Greece, and as a symbol of poetry soaring towards heaven. Later in the century Euphorion might have become a symbol of opera, the art-work of the future messianically uniting arts for-merly separate, a marriage (in Wagner's view), like that of Helena and Faust, between classical tragedy and the romantic symphony. In *Deutsche Kunst und Deutsche Politik* Wagner refers to the marriage of Helena and Faust as the highest calling of the German spirit, which King Ludwig of Bavaria had ordered to be celebrated in works of plastic art. For Wagner the union has become a wholly aesthetic arrangement. Helena is classical lucidity of form, Faust romantic ebullience of content. She is drama, disciplined and rigorous, he the invading subjectivity of music. Their offspring belongs in the prophetic future when the divided arts will regain their original unity: the spectral idea of opera vanishes on a horizon of perfection like Genius or Euphorion.

Goethe's extension of *Die Zauberflöte* is the bridge between it and Hofmannsthal, and the analogy is closer because *Die Frau ohne Schatten* also exists in two forms. As Goethe redeemed the pantomime of the opera in an allegory which has no need of music, so Hofmannsthal first produced his text in dramatic form for Strauss and then rewrote it as a long prose tale. In this case he is rescuing his own characters from the constrictions and externality of the drama, freeing them for the novel by endowing them with an interior life for which drama can find no correlative. The difference between the two versions illustrates Hofmannsthal's critical opposition between drama and the novel, which will be the center of the following chapter. Hofmannsthal saw opera on the analogy of the novel rather than on that of drama, as the next chapter will make clear, and this may explain his evident dissatisfaction with his allegory as musically dramatized by Strauss. Music and drama impose a necessary wilfulness on the characters, obliging them to register spiritual developments in large gestures and resounding climaxes, to do what Hamlet condemns and substitute theatrical swagger and prepared speeches for the difficult intimacy of the monologue. The novel permits them to find a way through their fears and longings privately, and silently. Penitentially anti-musical, Hofmannsthal's novelistic revision of *Die Frau ohne Schatten* imposes silence on the action, making the most crucial events occur in dumb-show, with very little speech, avoiding all concessions to the externality of opera.

Silence, the novelistic insistence on what the characters do not say, is a necessary restitution, because Strauss's music treats the allegory as science fiction, seizing the opportunity to fill the air with gaudy, unearthly sound. In Wagner the orchestra is a foundation

muttering and rumbling beneath the singers like a res-
tive volcanic substratum of the earth, surging and
swelling but also supporting the characters; the
Wagnerian orchestra is at Bayreuth sunk invisibly in a
pit and therefore functions as an internal, subliminal
commentary on the action. In Strauss music is not
beneath and therefore within the characters but around
and above them. In Wagner the music is a terrain in
which the characters are rooted, in Strauss an atmosphere in which they are enveloped. Strauss's element
is not earth or water—Wagner's mountains and
rivers—but air, in which Herod hears the beating of
the wings or Ariadne the cries of Bacchus, and through
which the Empress and the Nurse (who can flutter
round rooftops and negotiate chimneys) glide down to
the earth. The oriental extravagance of the score of *Die
Frau ohne Schatten,* with its tam-tams, Chinese gongs,
and glass harmonica, translates the allegory into exotic
fantasy. Hofmannsthal's second version rescues it
from Strauss, removing the occasions for grand operatic assertions and so freeing the characters from the
violent and deforming atmosphere of the music.

Music is intolerant of allegory, but so is the novel;
and in solving one problem Hofmannsthal creates
another for himself. Auden in his address at Salzburg
argued that novelistic characters, "people who are po-
tentially good and bad, capable of action and passivity," cannot exist in opera, because "music is immediate actuality and neither potentiality nor passivity
can live in its presence." Earlier, in a short piece in
*Vogue,* he had even taken a grim pleasure in calling *La
Bohème* unsatisfactory because Mimì is too long-
sufferingly passive, drifting into love with Rodolfo
and unobtrusively drifting away from him between

the acts. This is Hofmannsthal's difficulty when he expatriates his characters from opera. Their existence is no longer wilfully immediate; but nor can it become one of subjective potentiality, because they remain agents of an allegory who have little inside themselves to discover—their subjective existence is already rendered automatically in the tokens and prohibitions and way-stations of the allegory. They cannot be allowed to think for themselves, because their minds have been made up for them. Thus the Emperor is given no time to consider the meaning of the sung riddle at the entry of the magic cave: if he were to understand it, the encounter inside the cave and the suffering which follows would not be necessary.

Hence, in the retelling, the balance of the narrative is altered. The most passive character, the Emperor, assumes the center. Because it is his fate to be petrified into utter passivity, his only appearances in the opera are static moments of self-assertion, effusions of will: first as a hunter, then as a jealous husband, finally when restored to life jubilantly announcing the revocation of the curse. His developing is done in between these appearances on stage. Precisely for this reason, which is virtually a disqualification in opera, he is granted special prominence in the novel. He is the victim of the curse because his is the initial guilt. He assumed too self-confidently that he could win his bride over to humanity, but he is joined to her only by that physical exhilaration which makes him, as the Nurse says, a hunter and a lover and nothing more. Relying on power, he trusts to love to take her by force: besieging her with his attentions, he makes the same mistake as Barak in a different literary mode. The dyer's affection is too philanthropically all-embracing to be a compliment to his wife: the Emperor, having captured his wife during a hunt, continues to treat her as his prey, the patient object of his worshipful sexual aggression. For this reason he fails to engage her as his human equal and cannot loosen the knot of her heart. He is accustomed to lordly management (as the novel reveals in his brutal treatment of his falcon and falconmaster) and conceives of love as imperialism, demanding to know, for instance, how he can take possession of the unborn children forever. He must learn, as his daughter tells him, that the way towards rule is through service. Transformation to stone is apt punishment for the man of power, because it deprives him of power over himself. In the opera his weapons fail him at the falcon-house: he cannot use his arrow against his wife, because when it grazed the gazelle it released the woman; he cannot use his sword, because that loosed her girdle; and his hands are not capable of killing her. In the novel he is denied the use of his weapons and then of his hands, which stiffen numbly into stone: he reaches for his dagger to hurl at the girl whose wisdom offends him, but his fingers refuse to obey.

In the opera, because the Emperor's guilt belongs to the past history of his character and cannot be dramatized, because the Empress effaces herself in serving Barak and before the scene of judgment only confesses her guilt in asides, and because Barak's docile goodness makes him quietly accept whatever happens, the two initiating characters are Barak's wife and the Nurse. The wife is operatic because shrewish, forever exploding in spasms of rage which do not serve the action but only satisfy her temperament—the temperament, aptly, of a convulsively irritable and arrogant

opera singer, which was the profession of her prototype, Pauline de Ahna. The Nurse exists to work on
this furious temperament, to manufacture occasions
for its outbursts. She acts not only as tempter, but as
prompter.

In the novel, the Emperor as the unmoved mover of
the action, the individual whose transgression creates
the problem but who cannot save himself and must
await salvation by another, can become the center, and
the fourth chapter, treating events which have no place
in the opera, is given over to him. Here during his
search for the lost falcon he discovers his unborn children in a cave in the mountains, is entertained to a meal
by them and quizzes them on their identity. They re-
spond in riddles, and refuse to tell him how he can gain
possession of them, because at the moment when he
learns that he will drive them from him. The children
externalize his sense of guilt and enrage him by seem-
ing to flaunt secrets he dares not admit to himself: one
boy stares at him with the reproachful gaze of the
wounded falcon; the girl has the expression of the
gazelle in terror of its life. He hates them for the truths
they tell him about himself and reprimands them when
they begin to explain his wife's servitude to Barak. As
he raises his hand against them, he turns to stone, and
the children fade like flames, leaving him a statue alone
beneath the stars.

In the opera the Empress sees this happen in her
dream. In the novel it is her dream which the Emperor
overhears. The children chant her cry at him, "Dir,
Barak, bin ich mich schuldig!", their voices resounding in the vault of the cave like the chorus in the Grail
temple in *Parsifal*. Hofmannsthal's fourth chapter is a
recension not only of his text for the opera but also of

its model, *Die Zauberflöte,* which has the same defect of being unable to accompany Tamino and Pamina on their trials in the enchanted caves: Mozart reports on the trials by transcribing the music Tamino plays on the flute. The Emperor is Tamino with a psychological history, and for him allegory is no longer an arbitrary succession of marvels and curses but a secret and necessarily unmusical induction into moral and spiritual truth.

If Hofmannsthal writes the interior history of Mozart's characters, Auden writes their posterior, posthumous history, novelistically resurrecting them in the twentieth century. In 1956 he and Chester Kallman made a translation of *Die Zauberflöte* for NBC television. Translation inevitably became re-creation, a neoclassical correction of the naive Shakespearean collisions of the sublime and the nonsensical in Schikaneder's double plot. The antics of the cowardly Papageno during the trials are restrained, having been explained as interpolations by Schikaneder, the episodic comedian. Although Auden's sense of literary decorum is offended by the medley of suffering in Pamina's lament and self-congratulation in Papageno's clowning, his argument is rather with music than with literature, for it is music, specializing in emotional modulation, which justifies the impropriety of the double plot by acting out its ambiguities. The transitions between comedy and tragedy are managed by music: Strauss said he'd have given three of his operas to write those two bars in *Don Giovanni* when the minuet in which Leporello invites the maskers to the ball turns into the solemn trio in which they appeal for justice.

Auden's concern is to save the characters from

themselves, or at least from Schikaneder—to rescue, as Goethe wished to do in his continuation, the moral allegory from its association with joking and imposture. The spirit is to be liberated from the body; and as has been pointed out elsewhere, this was also the aim of romantic commentary on Shakespeare, which sought to translate plays, shabbily devoted to faking appearances, into novels, detesting show and preoccupied like Hamlet with what lies within, beyond the counterfeitings of the theater. Auden gives the Queen of the Night's dialogue to her three attendants, for the decorous reason that gods ought to sing, not stoop to conversation, and the prudential reason that the speaking voice of a coloratura soprano is seldom imposing. This is a characteristic device to extract the soul from the body after the fashion of Shakespeare's romantic apologists, to abstract the regal singing voice from the chirpy speaking voice. As implied by this romantic method of releasing the subjective secrets of character from the prison of fussy activity which constitutes the dramatic form, Auden sees the art of opera as a victory of spirit over nature. The victory is Faustian, achieved in defiance of natural limits, since the art of singing is a physical exertion which produces an exaltation of the spirit. The voice is a medium for striving, for accomplishing the impossible. Opera's apparent offences against realism positively boast of this, as Auden points out in his *Vogue* article: "How true to life . . . that out of two mountains of corseted flesh should issue such difficult and wonderful expressions of undying passion; that is what any really human love always is—and what a medium like the movies, which make love seem a natural effect caused by animal beauty, conceals—a triumph of Spirit over Nature."

Nature, in terms of the antithesis argued throughout this book, is the province of the drama, representing surfaces. Spirit belongs to the novel, which can probe emotional interiors.

As it is one of the rules of romantic commentary on Shakespeare that the characters are not exhausted by the actions the play requires of them but have a supernumerary life of spirit which invites imaginary sequels—their life is a novel from which a play excerpts only a few moments—so the *Magic Flute* of Auden and Kallman grants a posterior life to Sarastro and the Queen, who survive the opera and extend forward into our present. Sarastro speaks a metalogue between the acts, the Queen addresses a post-script to the impudent translators. The technique is that of *The Sea and the Mirror,* Auden's extension of *The Tempest,* a play which lies curiously on the edges of the concerns of this chapter: like *Faust* it turns drama into music, and Mozart apparently agreed to set it, to a libretto by F. H. von Einsiedel and F. W. Gotter, shortly before his death.

In Auden's version, Shakespeare's formalistic suppression of conflicts, made possible by the neat, symmetrical foreclosure of the dramatic form, is disputed by each of the truculent novelistic characters in turn. Prospero, who enforces a solution in the play, is unseated by Caliban. Taking over for himself the long-winded Jamesian periods in which Prospero has interpreted the past to Miranda, Caliban accuses Prospero, demanding, "Is it possible that, not content with inveigling Caliban into Ariel's kingdom, you have also let loose Ariel in Caliban's?" The suspicion is that the angel and the demon have changed places. Caliban is peremptorily absorbed into Prospero, who acknowl-

edges the thing of darkness as his own; Ariel correspondingly turns into a malign agent, the disruptive
force of poetry intruding upon the routine of reality,
"breaking down our picket fences in the name of
fraternity, seducing our wives in the name of romance,
and robbing us of our sacred pecuniary deposits in the
name of justice." Once out of captivity, Ariel has become both a libertine and a dangerous liberal.

The place-changing of Ariel and Caliban provides a
model for the cross-over of Sarastro and Astrafiammante in Auden's sequel to *Die Zauberflöte*. It is significant that he chooses to extract the pair of deities
rather than their human subjects, Tamino and Pamina,
on whom Goethe concentrates. Goethe is concerned
with apprenticeship, the *Lehrjahre* of those characters
whose struggle towards maturity spiritualizes the
picaresque form. The continuation is unfinished because there can be no end to the process of their
growth. To admit the possibility of an end is, as Faust
discovers, to fail. Auden deals, on the other hand, with
the spiritual managers of the action, who do not grow
but are, like gods, subject to metamorphosis instead.
They constantly change in appearance, but in essence
are always the same. Hence Auden's sequel is not
dramatic like Goethe's, since that would involve these
timeless beings in the shifts and compromises of time.
Rather Auden indicates the stasis in which they exist,
"eterne in mutabilitie" like Spenser's gods, by setting
them in the interstices of the dramatic action. Sarastro's place is between the acts, Astrafiammante's in the
postscript. They dwell in a limbo outside or adjacent to
the creation of Mozart and Schikaneder. Unanchored
in space, they are also safe from time and, as in Goethe
the persons of the allegory become aesthetic cate-
gories, Genius-Euphorion suggesting the idea of

opera, so these privileges make the two characters translators, surrogates in fact for Auden and Kallman. Translation is an art of spatial and temporal adjustment, crossing linguistic borders and bringing words and meanings up to date, and Sarastro and Astrafiammante are discovered making such adjustments, translating themselves from Europe to America and from 1791 to 1956. Translation removes a work of art from its context in space and time, making it both ubiquitous and immortal, and in doing so confers on it the status of a migratory, shape-changing god.

As Auden presents them, Sarastro and Astrafiammante adopt different stratagems of self-justification. Sarastro is an apologist for progress, democratizing the myth, suburbanizing the characters: he is the voice of benevolent American social hope. The Queen is a more sinister conservative, declaring that nothing ever changes because human nature is feeble and base, mistakenly trusted by democratic theorists: she is the underground, unregenerate voice of Mittel-Europa, making her appeal to instincts of aggression and regression. Whereas she speaks only for herself, Sarastro is anxious to identify the transformations the other characters, his charges, have undergone. They have crossed from beleaguered Europe to the tolerant protection of an American campus, where the Queen turns up as

> A highly paid and most efficient Dean
> (Who, as we all know, really runs the College)

and Sarastro himself becomes a dogged Casaubon

> tolerated for his knowledge
> Teaching the History of Ancient Myth

> At *Bryn Mawr, Vassar, Bennington* or *Smith.*

Tamino and Pamina have become exemplary graduate
students, she taking a job as a *Time* researcher to sub-
sidize his Ph.D. His trials are now domesticated rather
than fabulous: he proceeds

> Acquiring manly wisdom as he wishes
> While changing diapers and doing dishes.

The transformations of the Masonic temple into the
university, of theology into academic politics, of initiatic quests into degree courses and of the creed into a
study of anthropology, are brilliantly exact, for the
twentieth century has institutionalized and collec-
tivized the pilgrimage Tamino undertakes alone, and
his mental perils and lapses of faith have become the
intellectual uniform of every college student. The
search for wisdom is no longer lonely and forbidding,
fraught with difficult choices such as that Tamino
needs to make between the Queen and Sarastro; it is a
tour taken in the crowd of one's fellow students, and
the stages of one's approach to the goal are not obscure
but quantified in the form of grades. The triumphal
ending of the opera, in which wisdom and beauty as-
cend the throne while the chorus sings hymns, naturally would become the graduation ceremony.

Other fates await the characters who belong to the
biological rather than the mental world of the opera.
Kierkegaard had already singled out Papageno as representing one of the intermediate stages of the erotic,
lying between the indiscriminate dreaming desire of
Cherubino and the encyclopedic possessiveness of
Don Giovanni. In *Either/Or,* Kierkegaard too adopts
the characteristic nineteenth-century maneuvre of
separating the character, novelistically inexhaustible,
from enclosure in the drama through which it has con-

descended to pass: "It is important to separate the essential from the accidental, to conjure up the mythical Papageno and forget the actual person in the play." Dismissal of the person easily leads to dismissal of the work, and Kierkegaard indeed considers *Die Zauberflöte* unmusical because doctrinal rather than sensuous. This process of forgetting the person and then the work is one of translation and of mythopoeia. Kierkegaard contemptuously leaves "the actual Papageno" to his tedious consummation, which in fact is a realization of Caliban's dream of peopling the island with images of himself—Kierkegaard wishes him happiness in populating a primitive forest or a whole continent with Papagenos.

In describing the destiny of Papageno and Papagena, Auden perhaps follows a hint of Kierkegaard's, for while the other characters leave the sensuous field of music for the academic detachment of thought, this pair remains dependent on music:

> Sweet *Papagena,* when she's time to spare,
> Listens to *Mozart* operas on the air,
> Though *Papageno,* one is sad to feel,
> Prefers the juke-box to the glockenspiel.

Kierkegaard had argued that Tamino exists outside music, and that his flute-playing is tiresome and sentimental, whereas Papageno with his chiming bells and pipe is happily cocooned inside music, and his whole life is "an incessant twittering," as inane and contentless as bird-song. He dwells in the immediacy of sensation, while Tamino frets towards a future in consciousness which necessarily does away with music: the truth is first revealed to him, significantly, by a Speaker, who refuses the blandishments of song but

simply states the case against the Queen. Tamino
grows, Papageno merely recurs, and whenever he does
so he is always playing the same tune. Therefore it is
right for Auden to turn him from a maker of music
into a consumer of recorded music issuing from a
machine. His music is mediated through the juke-box,
as Papagena's is through the radio, because for them
music is an idle endless chirping accompaniment to
their activities, and because their new suburban existence alienates them from its sources. They constitute a
market for which music is turned out as merchandise.

The lecherous Moor remains a problem:

> And how is—what was easy in the past—
> A democratic villain to be cast?
> *Monostatos* must make his bad impression
> Without a race, religion or profession.

Monostatos loses from Sarastro's modernization,
since liberal ethics forbid him to be bad simply because
he is black and ugly, leaving him without a doctrine on
which to found his actions. Sarastro's embarrassment
recalls the difficulties of Shakespearean commentators
in apologizing for Shylock or Othello, or Wagner
critics on Mime and Beckmesser, whose wheedling,
whining accents were meant by the composer to
characterize what he felt to be the intolerable
cacophony of Jewish intonation, or on the black
gnome Alberich. Opera is a stronghold of will, and
therefore prejudice: democracy enfeebles it.

If Sarastro survives into the democratic age by astute
compromise, the Queen survives by sheltering underground, steadily augmenting her power throughout
the nineteenth century and waiting on the moment for
her return. She profits, as she points out, from roman-

ticism. Sneering at the final chorus of the opera, she demands

As for Wisdom and Beauty in heart-warming bliss,
Upon whom do they call every time that they kiss
But the blood-curdling Queen of the kingdom of Dis?

Romanticism contrived to reverse her relationship with Sarastro. The dour prophet of enlightenment becomes the enemy, Blake's tyrannical Newtonian god; his place in the temple is taken by the Queen, whose ferocity now seems to be the voice of elemental emotion, of the eternal delight of energy. She becomes a Blakean tigress. The icy pinnacles of her coloratura suggest the barbed vocal line of Anna in *Don Giovanni*, who was also turned by criticism into a heroine of furious, contradictory passion. As E. T. A. Hoffmann saw it, Anna's determination to destroy Don Giovanni was a reflex of her frustrated desire to become his spiritual partner, and this entanglement of revenge and love-longing points further towards the Isolde of Wagner's first act, the raging Irish sorceress who cannot forgive Tristan for making her love him. Romanticism joins Don Giovanni and Isolde as exemplars of opposite but complementary erotic myths, and the Queen makes herself the patroness of the union. Don Giovanni is the libertine racing against death to possess, fleetingly, every woman in the world: he recurs as the Zerbinetta of Strauss and Hofmannsthal. Isolde is the victim of emotion, not its cool profiteer, and for her sex is not a means of momentarily defeating death by miniaturizing it in the brief, endlessly repeatable death of erotic oblivion, but a chaste surrender to it: she recurs as Ariadne, welcoming Bacchus as the messenger of death. The Queen, claiming love as her own blood-curdling prerogative, presides over this irrational romantic marriage between the erotic and the deathly.

Her taunt is justified, for wisdom and beauty do acknowledge their helplessness in the war against her subliminal realm. The Lutheran chorale sung by the two armed men in *Die Zauberflöte* ushers in *Parsifal,* in which Mozart's action has a different conclusion. The fortress is no longer impregnable, because Sarastro in the person of Amfortas has already yielded to the Queen, the eternal Kundry. Tamino turns into the virginal fool Parsifal, without a Pamina because for him the awakening encounter is with the mother, who wishes both to corrupt him and to achieve her own redemption through him. Kundry collapses, as Nietzsche said all modern atheists did, at the foot of the cross. But for the Queen this is only a temporary setback, not a final defeat:

To that realm We descend when Our cue has been sounded
(Obedient to music) and there rule unbounded
Where your loves are enforced and your fantasies founded.

Schikaneder and Mozart clung to a hope a
Stage trap-door would bury this dark interloper,
But We'll never lack friends back in Mittel-Europa.

She then lists three of her apparitions, which span the romantic period and summarize this chapter. The first is "Goethe's Die Mutter, an understage chorus." Here at once there is a connection with Hofmannsthal, who identifies the realm of the Mothers, in an essay which will be more closely examined in the following chapter, as the origin of opera. It is from here that Faust produces the ideal image of Helena: here, buried in the collective unconsciousness of the race, lie the archetypes of all created beings, stored beyond the reach of time. As Mephistopheles describes them, they are surrounded by films of cloud which contain the patterns of all things which have been, are, or will be. Already it has been noted twice in this chapter that metaphysics tends to turn into aesthetics, that the allegory reveals itself to be about art—the union of Faust and Helena is an aesthetic alliance, and dialectically their offspring suggests the idea of opera; the Sarastro and Queen of Auden are translating gods, and translators of opera. The same aesthetic re-interpretation occurs in Hofmannsthal's references to the Mothers. The state of eternal suspension in which they exist becomes for him the mystic space of cultural history, the wall-less museum outside time where Homer, Shakespeare, and Rembrandt coexist as contemporaries and collaborators, just as the classical Helena can be found participating in the superstitious rites of the medieval world. The Mothers are the genii of formation and transformation, saving life (as Auden's translators save art) from stagnant completeness. For Hofmannsthal this becomes the synergism of the operatic form, in which different arts galvanize one another. Nietzsche traces the beginnings of opera to the cult of Dionysus; Hofmannsthal localizes it in the eclectic mythology of Goethe. In both territories the Queen presides.

Her next appearance is also from beneath the stage, but grudgingly: "Then for Wagner We half-rose as Erda." Goethe's myth and Wagner's are equalized here. Fed by the World-Spirit, the Mothers dwell at the center of the earth. It is from this depth that Erda, the mother of Brünnhilde and the Norns, sleepily rises in

*Das Rheingold* and *Siegfried* to chide Wotan for his conduct of the world, and it is to her that the Norns retire
as the dawn brightens in *Götterdämmerung,* despairing
of blind human wisdom. No longer the outlawed here-
tic of Mozart, the Queen has promoted herself to the
voice of universal wisdom, a spirit of foreknowledge
and judgment, reversing the conclusion of *Die Zauberflöte*. She has the nonchalance and the dangerous re-
silience of all mythological characters, blandly undertaking to transform herself into her opposite while
remaining insidiously the same.

Her final accession of power occurs when

> for Us
> Freud adds a blunt synonym to the Thesaurus,

excavating that gloomy space under the stage where
she lies in wait (Wagner's sunken trench for the subliminal orchestra, or the vast mental space which
Hofmannsthal, in the essay on Shakespeare, says we all
have within us) and turning it into a communal pit of
morbid fantasy in which we are all imprisoned.
Psychology confirms the Queen's reign by establishing a dictatorship of instinct.

Auden's interpretative miracle is to have made the
gods change both places and values. In the opera, the
Queen's dizzy coloratura makes her a creature of the
heights, while Sarastro's somber and resonant hymns
emerge from a grave, bottomless depth. Though they
never meet, they confront each other across this distance like the spirits, some hovering in the air, some in
caverns, in the final scene of *Faust*. But just as Auden
can make Caliban speak the hypotactic language of
Ariel, so in his continuation the Queen no longer
blazes among the stars, but has withdrawn to subter-

ranean psychological depths, while Sarastro's fate is to have been elevated to a powerless academic eminence.

The metamorphoses studied in this chapter follow a course similar to that described earlier in Shakespeare's case: in liberating an allegory from Schikaneder's confused text they point the work beyond opera. As with the musical Shakespeare, there is an interpretative passage from drama to novel in all the adaptations treated. Goethe and Hofmannsthal remove the characters into a spiritual future, Kierkegaard discovers in them a potential psychological future, and Auden records their migratory social future, in exploratory epilogues which stretch the closed, enigmatically terse drama into the likeness of a novel, a form with the leisure in time and amplitude in space to pursue their interior adventures. These epilogues introduce the subject of the next chapter, which is precisely the adjustment of theory to remake opera, mistakenly considered musical drama, as a musical novel.

# 4. The Operatic Novel

When the Rostovs visit the opera in *War and Peace,*
Natasha coldly notes the grotesque unreality of the
scene, ashamed at the imposture but sardonic as well at
the expense of the shabby artifice of cardboard and
glue, the semaphoric arm-waving, the attitudinizing
and courting of applause, the swarm of acrobatic men
and women with bare legs. Opera has reduced drama
to a final pitiable absurdity. Natasha knows she is
watching a meretricious cheat. The supposed lovers
ignore one another to bow to the public, the distracted
maiden has the self-possession to manage several
changes of costume, a devil sings and gesticulates until
suddenly a trap-door opens and he plunges beneath the
stage. Drama has become an image of cynical decep-
tion and bad faith, and it is exposed as such by the small
alarms of novelistic spontaneity which crowd the
"entr'actes"—the appearance of Pierre, sad but
stouter, Kuragin's gaze, Natasha's blush, and Ana-
tole's pressure on her arm. Drama is shamed by these
starts of unpremeditated feeling, which are the prerogative of the novel.

Romanticism came to insist ever more exclusively
on the opposition between drama and the novel: between external action in a crampingly compact form
and subjective exploration in a limitlessly ramifying
form. But as this happens, opera defends itself from
disapproval like Natasha's by moving away from the
drama towards the novel.

This may have been its destiny from the first. Wagner's formula of music–drama slides over the enmity between its components. As music is often the enemy of words, drowning their sense in lyrical sound, so it is liable to act against the interests of drama, slowing down action while rendering it sentimentally internal. Opera is inefficient as drama simply because it takes so much longer to sing a phrase than to say it. But, novelistically, this may be its justification, for in extending the phrase it allows its characters time to reflect on and absorb the implications of what they are uttering. Ambiguously accompanied by music, the multiple repetitions of one another's names by Tristan and Isolde have a constantly varying significance which they could never have in drama.

Music tends to subdue and inundate its text, and this confirms opera's adherence to the novel. For as music invades a text, it re-enacts the process Schopenhauer discerned in the creation of a novel. He made it a rule that a novel would be the finer the more it concentrated on inner life to the exclusion of that outer life which belonged to the dramatist, and even proposed that the ratio between internal and external might be a means of computing a novel's excellence. *Tristram Shandy,* for instance, was perfect, as *Tristan und Isolde* may be said to be, because it had no action at all. From the first, opera has conceded that music can probe states of mind but not advance actions. The formal balance of eighteenth century opera virtually institutionalizes this conflict between drama and novel: plot is dealt with in the brisk gabble of recitative, while in the arias music intervenes to describe a static condition of spirit.

In setting words, opera obscures them by transmuting them into notes. In providing music to accompany

9. Wagner disembodied: Jean Delville's "Tristan and Yseult," 1887.

a drama, it subverts that drama into a sentimental or psychological novel.

These paradoxes preoccupy Hofmannsthal in critical essays which unwittingly prepare for his collaboration with Strauss, since they look towards music as the redeemer of literature and insist on a necessary interfusion of the arts. The present chapter will attempt to relate this early literary criticism to Hofmannsthal's later practice as an operatic librettist. Hofmannsthal envisages the victory of music as a triumph of the novel over drama. In the Weimar address of 1905 on Shakespeare's kings and nobles, he attempts to define the unifying impression which is the sum of all the separate plays when they merge and disappear into one another in a universal novel, and this whole he feels to be musical: a symphony of lamenting sound, "eine tief ergreifende, feierlich-wehmütige Musik." *Henry VIII* is compared with a Beethoven sonata: in it festivity and mourning interpenetrate, and the Shakespearean double plot is transposed into the sonata method of thematic development.

Hofmannsthal sees it as the destiny of words to surrender to music in Shakespeare's romantic comedies, where dramatic conflicts are subdued by a musical harmony. At the same time, a surrender to dance occurs as well, anticipating the subject of Salome in the final chapter, for these comedies end in hymeneal dances whose symmetry is an image of the order of generation. They prefigure what Hofmannsthal calls, in his piece of 1905 on Wilde's final incarnation as Sebastian Melmoth, "the dance of life." Dance absorbs drama in his own *Elektra*. Here the comic patterning of Shakespeare's jigs has given way to a tragic convulsion, but the progress from the dance as an image of comic social cohesion to the dance as an image of the fierce, deranging power of natural impulse is logical. Hofmannsthal implies as much in quoting Dschellaledim Rumi at the end of the Wilde essay—he who knows the power of the dance of life does not fear death, because he knows that love kills. This is precisely what Elektra tells Chrysothemis in their exultant duet before her dance of macabre celebration. As Strauss set it, that dance preserves a certain ambiguity in its odd tragic-comedy; she is both a rampaging maenad and a Viennese waltzer transfigured and out of control. Hofmannsthal remembers a similar moment of uncertainty in Beerbohm Tree's production of *Twelfth Night*. As it ends, couples join hands and antagonisms are appeased, but a shadow crosses this dance, the dark recollection of the other equalizing ritual of the "Totentanz."

Although Shakespeare is admitted to possess a sovereign power over language, what matters for Hofmannsthal is his music, which lies beyond words. Literary attention is fixed on the individual diversities of the plays, but this music can only be apprehended in the Whole, "das Ganze," in an all-comprehending, climactic play which Shakespeare did not in fact write (but which the romantics compose on his behalf). That summary play, which exists in uncreated silence, is a species of musical novel, for Hofmannsthal's description of it connects with E. M. Forster's notion, in *Aspects of the Novel,* of a novel's expansion into the "common entity, this new thing, . . . the symphony as a whole." Expansion is the moment at which time becomes space, when after the orchestra has played Beethoven's Fifth Symphony all its movements retrospectively enter the mind at once and "we hear something that has never actually been played." As, in Hofmannsthal's view, the words in Shakespeare's plays long for the silence of the play he never wrote, so, in Forster's argument, the form of a novel or a symphony can only acquire significance after the work is over, when it has a silence to reverberate in. Rhythm, the musical idea which Forster appropriates for the aesthetics of the novel, can only be perceived in the intervals between its beats.

This law of form had already been proclaimed in d'Annunzio's novel *Il fuoco*. There, a group of Wagnerian enthusiasts insists that the essence of music lies not in the sounds themselves but in the silence that precedes and follows them, and that rhythmic throbs are inaudible except in the pauses between sounds. Stelio Effrena in this novel also invokes the example of Beethoven, imagining "the interval between two scenic symphonies in which all the motifs unite to express the inner essence of the characters that are struggling in the drama and to reveal the inner depths of the action, as, for instance, in Beethoven's great prelude in *Leonore* or in *Coriolanus*." That pregnant silence constitutes an atmosphere in which poetry can be created and character conceived, since the personages of drama will "emerge from the symphonic ocean as if from the truth itself of the hidden being that operates within them," and everything they say will expand into meaning because there is a rhythmic silence for it to reverberate in, and "because it will be animated by a continual aspiration to song that cannot be appeased except by the melody that shall rise again from the orchestra at the end of the tragic episode." Tragic significance resides not in the drama but in the musical intervals which interrupt it and in the silence before and after it.

Stelio Effrena clings, all the same, to the form of the drama. But Forster applies the same notion of the work which expands rather than being completed, which liberates its component parts in "the rhythm of the whole," to the novel, not to drama. Being less attached to characters, drama extends in the opposite direction, away from music towards painting which, Forster implies, imposes a disciplined and limiting form, puts a frame round the action. The novel's alliance is with music, which admittedly "does not employ human beings" but may become novelistic in making the orchestra an image of consciousness, of thought overheard. Thus is is not the words of Tristan and Isolde we trust in the first act, but their thoughts as the orchestra confides them—not the dramatic situation of conflict and contempt but the secret, subversive, novelistic situation of mutual longing which is musically intimated in the prelude, before any words can intrude.

As has been seen in the commentary on the two versions of *Die Frau ohne Schatten,* Hofmannsthal found a practical difficulty in the incompatibility of dramatic character, which is external, free-standing and active, and novelistic character, which is internal, intimate, and passive. For him as for Forster only the latter was truly musical. But it was musical without being operatic. Bragging, wilful, and violent, operatic characters are in this sense not musical at all. It is not heroic singing which makes Tristan and Isolde musical, but the confessions made on their behalf by the orchestral introductions to the first and third acts. Wagner derives a telling irony from the contradiction of drama by novel. As participants in a drama, Tristan upholds the chivalric formalities and Isolde rehearses the official history of the wrongs done to her. But beneath this level of public responsibility, in the psychological novel which develops in the sunken and invisible orchestra pit, they are infatuated with one another. For Hofmannsthal, however, the differences between drama and novel remain problematical.

Even in the criticism which predates his alliance with Strauss, he reveals a disposition to treat literary details as pictorial images or musical themes, as if with faltering confidence in the independence of literature. For instance, if *Twelfth Night* is considered dramatically, divisions remain at the end: partners are exchanged with implausible glibness, and Malvolio abstains from the dance, promising revenge. But in Hofmannsthal's musical reading of the play this dramatic differentiation of character is obscured, and personal destinies are of no more significance than "a single fleck of color on an ornament or a detached theme in a long musical work." The musical whole Hofmannsthal praises requires, it becomes clear, the destruction of the drama. Characters in Shakespeare are reduced to parity with sounds in Beethoven or colors in Rubens, abstract and malleable materials of art, not ambassadors from the human world outside art. They exist in order to be transformed into atmosphere, which Hofmannsthal feels to be "ein ungeheures Ensemble," as inextricable as the atmosphere of spring, and they are stifled by it. Shakespeare permits them to contest the totalitarian whole, as Falstaff quarrels with military ethics or Hamlet with the procedures of revenge. But Hofmannsthal's musical ensemble is indivisible and tolerates no dissent or discord. The "individual freedom" which Forster says the notes and tunes find in the rhythmic whole is, if compared with the disputatious independence Shakespeare's characters enjoy, not freedom but imprisonment: or rather that dubious Hegelian freedom which resides in acquiescence to necessity.

Elsewhere, Hofmannsthal sees the characters as subject to an abstract order of color. Shakespeare's young men, he says, have no other purpose than the glorification of life, and they are placed in the design as if they were bright areas of red and yellow in a painting. Literature is undergoing reduction to the contentlessness of music and non-representational painting: it is being made to aspire to the condition of opera, where words exist only to be submerged in or distorted by music. This flight from literature into music, painting, and dance will be more fully discussed in the next chapter in the case of *Salome,* the work which immediately preceded Strauss's partnership with Hofmannsthal.

Hofmannsthal returns to the antagonism between drama and the novel in his essay on Balzac. He distinguishes Balzac's characters from epic individuals like Odysseus, Lear, or Quixote by saying that those are immortally complete in their gestures, dramatically separate from their backgrounds, whereas each individual in Balzac is enmeshed in an atmospheric whole, never granted independence from this enveloping organism of society. This interdependence he conceives of as pictorial and/or musical. On the one hand, he says it is as impossible to isolate details as in a picture by Rembrandt or Delacroix. On the other, he calls Balzac's persons single notes contributing to a gigantic symphony.

In the imaginary dialogue between Balzac and Hammer-Purgstall, Hofmannsthal sets the novelist himself to demarcate his own characters from those of the stage. Balzac fends off Hammer-Purgstall's request

that he write a play by wondering if his people could
survive the stage, for, unlike Shakespeare, he does not,
he reveals, believe in "characters." In the theater,
characters are allotropic phenomena, crystallizations
of real persons who lie outside art, or else contrapuntal
necessities, and Hofmannsthal's Balzac declares himself interested in the chemical process rather than in the
crystals which form as a result of it, in destinies, not in
persons. He refers to his characters as litmus paper,
which is automatically turned red or blue by the acids
of powers or fates; and it is the novel's task to represent
the subjective operation of process rather than the ob-
jective theatrical business of product and reaction. To
exchange Hofmannsthal's chemistry for D. H. Lawrence's geology, the novelist's interest is in the carbon,
the dramatist's in the diamond.

The implication for the libretti Hofmannsthal was
to write is that he saw opera as a musical novel rather
than musical drama, dealing in psychological change
and shifts of consciousness, not endeavor and
achievement. Wherever possible he rescues characters
from the epic or dramatic sources which require them
to conquer and to brave catastrophes, and transports
them to the novel, where they can work out their destinies in self-communing silence. *Ariadne auf Naxos*
and *Die Ägyptische Helena* both translate the busy,
commanding characters of myth into suffering passivity. Ariadne lies prone and still, awaiting her transformation, and when Bacchus arrives it is not as the new
lover saluted by Zerbinetta—who, with her partners,
wanders through this world of novelistic subjectivity
as an unregenerate representative of drama, the
frivolous and wordly drama of the "commedia
dell'arte"—but as a change in her awareness of herself.
As Hofmannsthal explained in a letter to Strauss, Bac-

chus discloses to Ariadne the depths of sorcery in her own nature. Likewise, in the later work, Hofmannsthal revives the legend of Helena's sojourn in Egypt while the Greeks and Trojans fought over a visionary facsimile of her and uses it to reconvert myth into psychology, exposing the epic clash of armies as no more than a phantasmagoria.

Dramatic myth is again dissolved into novelistic psychology in *Elektra,* in this case by way of the transformation of Greek tragedy into Freudian therapy. While the Greeks of Gluck's operas are those of Winckelmann, lucid, still, calmly grand, those of Strauss and Hofmannsthal are the Greeks of Nietzsche, agonized, accursed and hysterical. Nietzsche's interpretation of Greek culture had been extended in Freud's psychoanalysis of Oedipus, and *Elektra* joins Nietzsche and Freud. Strauss's erupting, overbearing score dramatizes the merciless oppression of natural forces which, for Nietzsche, lies at the source of Greek myths: it is Dionysian music, turning pain into ecstasy. Hofmannsthal's text, on the contrary, adopts the Apollonian method of diagnosis: it modifies the analytical procedures of Greek tragic interrogation and makes Elektra the physician who is herself more diseased than her patients. Klytemnestra comes to Elektra to describe her symptoms and to have her dreams interpreted, but the remedy Elektra prescribes is the axe. For Elektra, the cure is equally fatal: she is destroyed when relieved of her obsession. In their final duet, Elektra and Chrysothemis sing radiantly of Nietzsche's view of the Greeks, transfigured by suffering, but their joy is at once analyzed in the Freudian way as a fever of the mind, and Elektra's dance of triumph is the onset of mania.

Although Elektra belongs in tragic drama, Hofmannsthal subdues her to a novelistic passivity by making her weak and incapable, desperately reliant on others. Like Hamlet, she is a character unequipped to participate in drama, a monologuist, not an activist. Though he is more usually linked with the Freudian Oedipus, Hamlet is, like Elektra, a specialist in morbid anatomy who passes the time of the play in verbal sound and fury while the actions he dreams of are initiated by others. The idea of revenge interests him, but not the act. Elektra likewise is possessed by an idea, prolonging her state of brooding despair and unable to recover once it is terminated. She prophesies revenge and celebrates it, but cannot perform it. Her need is for an agent, and throughout the work she searches for a dramatic deputy to whom she can pass on her mission. But just as Hamlet invents situations in art while others seize opportunities in life, so each of her attempts at aggression or initiation is rebuffed. Her victory over Klytemnestra is verbal only and is cut short by the message about Orest's death. When next Chrysothemis rejects her, Elektra delivers a curse which is a cry of anguished ineffectualness rather than a climax of self-assertion. The eventual appearance of Orest, which Elektra has so impatiently anticipated, brings only shame, as if she were happier to treasure him in private as an actor in her vindictive fantasy rather than to see her wish fulfilled. Her celebration of his entry into the house, like her dance around Aegisth, is a grotesque and time-wasting irelevance, an imaginative ritual which retards the action as Hamlet's theatricals do. Orest's tutor scares her off by rebuking them for making so much noise, and leads him inside to perform the deed Elektra can only talk about. She even forgets to give him the axe she has kept for him.

10. The passive Elektra: Birgit Nilsson in Paris, 1974.

Inaction is, as Salvador Dali says, a mode of irony, and this is true of Elektra, ferociously impotent as she is. But the analytical, novelistic irony of Hofmannsthal's text is here contradicted by the dramatic hysteria of Strauss's music. The text is riddling, intricate, secretive, a tense exploration of images and private obsessions. Its Apollonian and therapeutic task of converting mania into character analysis is hampered by the Dionysian eruptions of the score.

Hofmannsthal's people soliloquize. Conversations can only proceed by neurotic cross-purpose, with characters pursuing personal demons and failing to notice that each is interpreting the subject of discussion quite differently. Here again a Greek dramatic procedure turns Freudian and novelistically internal. Greek dramatic irony is structural, a factor of the audience's superior knowledge of the fable; Hofmannsthal's conversations deflect it into a psychological irony, as parallel fantasies develop beyond the possibility of convergence. Elektra and Klytemnestra are describing two quite different kinds of sacrificial victim. Elektra and Aegisth are anticipating two quite different kinds of welcome inside the house. Elektra and Chrysothemis sing together of two quite different kinds of love.

But whereas the text individualizes, music identifies. Voices overlap and blend, even while saying quite incompatible things. The orchestral setting can only be a glorious immolation of the text. Strauss's volcanic score invades the novelistic privacy of Hofmannsthal's people, whose monologues are now populated, accompanied by the cacophonous efforts of a hundred or more musicians. Their declamations are now belligerently public. Characters who are in Hof-

mannsthal neurasthenic casualties are made invulnerable by their vocal contest with the orchestra.

Still, Elektra as much as Salome needs music.
Neither heroine is content with verbal drama, with
mere recitation. Music acts out Elektra's fantasies, accompanying her triumphal waltzes with a jubilant din,
just as it gives immediate realization to Salome's erotic
wishes when, after Jokanaan's return to the cistern, the
orchestra tempts her to demand his head. But theirs
ought to be the "music unheard" of Keats, silent psychological music, not the brazen tumult of Strauss.
When Chrysothemis asks if she hears the musical up-
roar honoring Orest, Elektra corrects her, saying that
the music comes from within her.

Virtually desiring the musical destruction of his
text, Hofmannsthal follows these heroines in search-
ing for a coalition of forms. At the end of the lecture on
Shakespeare he describes the composite art-work as
one in which the various arts will combine to reclaim a
mythic unity they have forfeited during the long degeneration in which art ceased to be an instrument of
worship and prophecy and was a trivialized into enter-
tainment.

The synesthesia which prompts Hofmannsthal to
treat Balzac as a painter and a musician finds its justification here. He admits that his aim in the lecture on
Shakespeare was to propose a merger between three
primeval artistic forces—the Atmosphere of Shakespeare, the Chiaroscura of Rembrandt, and the Myth
of Homer.

Atmosphere and Chiaroscura are equivalent properties. Shakespeare's characters are not fixed in isolation
around the points of a zodiac like Dante's, but are
joined to one another; they stand out from the element

which contains them, as men, angels, and beasts do in
the pictures of Rembrandt. Chiaroscura for Hofmannsthal is pictorial atmosphere, a medium which
inter-involves all living creatures. In literary terms, it is
a property of the novel, since Hofmannsthal has argued that drama must separate characters gesturally,
whereas novels like those of Balzac entwine them in
the atmosphere and the subtle shades of their society.

The third property is Myth, which, as Eliot said of
*Ulysses,* reduces to significance the bewildering
plenitude of modern life. The union Hofmannsthal
envisages between these three faculties will, he says,
provide the talisman, the magic formula with which
the artist will be able to evade both space and time and
descend to the Mothers, there to create the work of art
the age longs for, one which makes an atmosphere for
its existence, sets its characters moving in the chiaroscura of life, and injects it with myth. Although Hofmannsthal does not say so, this work must by implication be an opera. Wotan's task, at once philosophical
and political, of creating a hero who is independent of
divine will and can therefore serve it, has devolved on
the artist: he is now the god who must release the age,
as Hofmannsthal says, from its plight. In Wagner the
superman is the art-work of the future; in Hofmannsthal the metaphysical paradox which is the superman
turns back into a prescription for the futuristic formal
paradox of opera.

Hofmannsthal's glowing key which unlocks the
way down to the Mothers derives from *Faust* but, as
the previous chapter has noted, it also suggests the
descent of the Norns as day dawns in *Götterdämmerung*.
They retreat, safeguarding their wisdom, from the errant human world to the immemorial stasis where

Erda awaits them. As Hofmannsthal takes up the legend and translates it into literary criticism, the entranced artist follows them, avoiding the threat of
daylight and contemporaneity, seeking instead what
Nietzsche called "the mythic womb." Metaphysics
becomes aesthetics: the artist outstrips space and time
by overcoming the limits they impose on the separate
arts, fusing music and poetry, which are time-bound,
with the spatial and scenic forms of the stage. Forster's expansion is also a moment of aesthetic mysticism, when as in Hofmannsthal's formula space and
time are fused.

The conjunction of Shakespearean Atmosphere
with Rembrandtian Chiaroscura and Homeric Myth
can readily be translated into a project for opera. The
circumambient atmosphere which contains characters,
the mystically alive space between them as Hofmannsthal calls it, is the music, discovering a subjective affin-
ity between those who, like Tristan and Isolde, imag-
ine themselves opposed. Chiaroscura becomes the
province of the scenic designer and the lighting techni-
cian, who make the stage a painting which moves. At
the moment in *Parsifal* when Gurnemanz announces
that space has become time, Wagner makes the scenery
start to walk. After the experiments of Adolphe Appia,
light took on the function of emotional dramatization.
In the Bayreuth productions of Wieland Wagner
people were kept hieratically still, while the lights playing over them suggested motion and change. Birgit
Nilsson once said of Wieland, "He could make people
look sixteen or seventeen just by changing the lights."
Personal identity, that is, becomes fluid in the lights
and is remade. Character is both submerged in the
musical atmosphere, and softened and made malleable

by light. This double process of dissolution is also a reversion to myth, since the character thus eroded by music and light becomes an incident in the collective unconsciousness, roving through space and time like Kundry, whose metamorphoses Klingsor refers to, or Salome, whose wanderings will be the subject of the following chapter.

The necessity of myth preoccupied Hofmannsthal. Discussing *Die Ägyptische Helena* with Strauss, he insisted that mythological opera was the truest of forms and refused to adopt, as Strauss wished, the bourgeois method of realistic dialogue. But if myth is rediscovered in the descent to the Mothers, there is a danger that the depths to be plumbed may turn out be bathetic rather than profound, and in Hofmannsthal's texts there is a constant self-protective admission of bathos in the glib convertibility of characters and situations between myth and comic actuality. In his explication of *Ariadne,* Hofmannsthal describes Circe, from whom Bacchus escapes, as a demonized Zerbinetta. His first intention was to make the earthly pair in *Die Frau ohne Schatten* characters from the "commedia dell'arte"; then he translated them into Viennese urban types speaking in dialect; at last he rendered them allegorical, endowing Barak with the emblematic trade of dyer, making him work in the impure matter of human affection as against the frail, vitreous colorlessness of the Empress. The series of conversions admits the myth to be conscious fabrication, invented rather than recovered from the deeps, oddly baseless and provisional.

Fissures run through all of Hofmannsthal's insecure myths. His correspondences are conceits, like the wail of the frying fish which is the protest of the children denied birth: they are strained efforts to prove a connection rather than mystic disclosures of a relationship. They belong in that skeptical phase when myth is failing and has to be patched up as allegory. There is an analogy to the complaining fish in another work written in the hiatus between myth and the experimental fables of allegory, Spenser's *The Faerie Queene*. In the generative Garden of Adonis (Book III, Canto VI) unborn, uncouth forms are planted in comely rows of seed beds, and importunate, naked babes cluster around old Genius, the porter who mans the gate leading into the world, demanding to be attired with fleshly weeds.

Allegory replaces character by conception. This is why the unborn children are so central to the novelistic version of *Die Frau ohne Schatten,* for like Spenser's babes they are literally conceptions, awaiting a later material incarnation as characters. While identity becomes molten in light, character comes to reside in shadows: the struggle of the Empress to cast a shadow is her quest for material embodiment as a character. But the image remains a damagingly ambiguous one. The shadow is thin, insubstantial, an accessory rather than an embodiment of natural life. Hofmannsthal can only preserve the secretive novelistic subjectivity of the fable by choosing as the token of human fertility something which seems to mean the opposite. The shadow is empty and infertile, and Ariadne even uses it as an image of painful vacancy of mind—in her depression, "Nur Schatten streichen durch einen Schatten hin," only shadows slip through a shadow.

In Hofmannsthal's theory myth solidifies character. In practice it contributes to the etiolation of character, further wasting its substance. The defensive, disarming self-criticism of Hofmannsthal's texts even prompts him to question the integrity of his own myths. Thomas Mann's Leverkühn in *Doktor Faustus* asks why all the methods and conventions of contemporary art are good for parody only, and disintegrative ironic parody lies at the center of most of the operas of Strauss and Hofmannsthal. Ochs coarsely parodies the Marschallin's refined and discreet adultery. Zerbinetta mocks Ariadne and taunts the Composer who writes the work. Elektra neurotically parodies the act of revenge someone else must perform for her. The analogy with *Die Zauberflöte* introduces the suspicion of parody into *Die Frau ohne Schatten,* in the contrast between the airy intelligence of the spirit-beings and the grotesque squabbling, gorging, and toiling of the lower people. The Empress, as has been noted in the previous chapter, even confesses an atavistic longing to become Papagena.

Wagner had earlier recognized that state of the decrepitude of myth when it turns into parody in designing the mercantile song-auction in *Die Meistersinger* as a parody of the trial in the Wartburg from *Tannhäuser.* But this at least reproduced the duality of the Greek dramatic festivals, in which a tragedy was followed by a satyr-play. It also ironically demonstrated that while in the age of faith art is the servant of religion, in the age of commerce art becomes a religion and is coveted by tradesmen as a means of redemption from their grubby and prosaic existences. Wagner also granted the tragedy priority. History in the age of faith is tragedy, in the age of commerce, farce.

Hofmannsthal, however, begins with parodic exposure and then expects tragedy to rescue the situation from his disdain. He begins by shattering the illusion but then demands that we believe in it all the more trustingly. In *Ariadne* the heroine is at first the capricious prima donna, refusing to share the stage with sordid comedians and petitioning for cuts in the tenor's music. Immediately afterwards, she pours forth what Hofmannsthal calls "the monologue of her lonely soul" and suffers through the miracle of a return to life. The tenor of the prologue, strutting in his panther-skin and boxing the wig-maker's ears, changes as we watch into a redeeming god. Sham becomes imaginative transformation. Myth is abraded by the idea of performance, its impostures and its interruptions, and the sheer shame of the theater. The result is a charade. All that is left of the gods is their costumes, which vain opera singers try on for effect. These are the latter-day metamorphoses of the gods: Ariadne is no longer herself but a Marschallin between lovers; Bacchus is no longer the son of Venus but a self-possessed Hanswurst indulging in a tantrum.

Hofmannsthal's prescription for the composite art-work is confident enough. Homer, Shakespeare, and Rembrandt are to be brought together as if in the wall-less museum of André Malraux, and this artificial contiguity of different arts and epochs will produce the opera. In comparison with Wagner's imperial notion of himself as the triple reincarnation of Aeschylus, Shakespeare, and Beethoven, Hofmannsthal's formula has something of the academic quality of Forster's fantasy in *Aspects of the Novel*, which sets all the novelists of the past two centuries to work side by side in the British Museum reading room. Wagner had turned the theater into a temple consecrated to the worship of his own art; Strauss and Hofmannsthal, paying an envious tribute to the past in the form of pastiche, turn it into a museum stocked with the venerable works of others.

The juxtaposition of Homer, Shakespeare, and Rembrandt in the museum of cultural history suggests the reconstitution of the past in a work like *Der Rosen-kavalier,* where Mozartean comedy and Wagnerian tragedy, or the Vienna of the rococo and Maria Theresa and the Vienna of the waltz and the operetta, are superimposed. The Wagnerian myth of erotic yearning is translated to a comically worldly Mozart-ean society. The Marschallin is an Isolde who has learned the comic art of survival, and she relies not on magic, like Isolde, but on manners to save herself. *Der Rosenkavalier* begins with a parody of Wagner, in the orgiastic exultation of the prelude (Wagner never permits physical satisfaction: the sex in his works is always coitus interruptus) and Oktavian's complaint against the daylight. These social beings have taken Wagner's metaphors literally: Tristan's objection to the tiresome obligations of daylight consciousness is answered by Oktavian's drawing the curtains. Their night of love concludes with breakfast. The Marschal-lin and Oktavian discuss the philosophical problems of identity which perplex Tristan and Isolde—"Was heisst das 'Du'? Was 'du und ich'?"—but whereas Tristan and Isolde exchange names and selves and be-come one another, the Marschallin and Oktavian ex-change erotic pet-names, Bichette and Quinquin. They are at once Mozart's Countess and Cherubino, embroiled in intrigue and cautionary disguise, and Wagner's lovers aching with rapture. *Ariadne* is another work of quizzical superimposition: although the patron's demand that the opera and the episodic comedy be run together horrifies the Composer, it allows Hofmannsthal once again to make different periods of the past simultaneously and quarrelsomely present and allows Strauss to urge a delicate chamber orchestra to strain in raucous tribute to the love duet which concludes *Siegfried.*

These are works engaged in a shame-faced debate on the possibility of their own existence. They have that self-interrogatory anxiety which has increasingly overtaken modern works of art, making them ask whether they can live down their internal divisions or whether they dare claim to be art at all. In this respect the sequel to the joint works of Strauss and Hofmannsthal is *Capriccio,* for which Clemens Krauss provided the text. This is an opera about the possibility of opera, about the friction between notes and words. The antagonism in *Ariadne* is between characters who belong in different genres. The antagonism in *Capriccio* is more disruptive, because it is between the elements which constitute the work of art.

*Ariadne* incites the tensions which the double plots of Mozart conceal into open disagreement. Shakespeare, as Johnson says, forces the mourner and the reveller, the tragic and the heedlessly comic, into proximity, and Mozart does the same, interweaving the trials of Tamino with the antics of Papageno, allowing the lighter people (as Malvolio would call them) to rejoice in Don Giovanni's destruction and then repair to the inn for a drink. Tamino and Don Giovanni generously tolerate the comedians, but *Ariadne* dismantles Mozart's tragicomedy by setting the opposed groups of characters to dispute control of the stage. It is a work of curiously astringent nostalgia, asserting the impossibility of the form it lovingly imitates. There is a knowing vacuousness to it: Tamino accepts Papageno as part of himself, Don Giovanni incorpo-

rates Leporello because their ambitions are the same
and the difference is merely one of style, but in *Ariadne*
tragedy and comedy call each other's bluff. Neither
believes in the other. Ariadne is not genuinely tragic;
nor is Zerbinetta (who presents herself to the Composer as a forlorn and bereft Ariadne, the victim of her
own theatrical impostures, but who is for Hofmannsthal an insidious enchantress, a more benign Circe)
genuinely comic. Each turns the other into a parody
and a cheat. The Composer disowns his work, and in a
recent production by Jean-Pierre Ponnelle in Cologne
returned at the end during the fireworks to blow his
brains out.

*Ariadne* is a work of art gone wrong, but *Capriccio*
doubts whether it can claim to be a work of art at all.
Despite its consuming aestheticism, it remains skeptical about art. Like the late novels of Henry James, it
renders all emotions aesthetic—matter is finally eliminated by form, and all experiences, eating, talking,
making love, become subject to the rarified discipline
of art. The characters are words and notes, not people.
Flamand calls "Ton und Wort" brother and sister, and
questions of family and erotic attraction are translated
throughout into an aesthetic debate. But although the
accidents and informalities of life have been banished,
what is left is not a pure and perfect formalistic artifact
but a querulous and indecisive work which solves the
problem of rivalry between words and music only by
arranging a stalemate. Rather than choose between
Olivier and Flamand, the Countess sends them to meet
one another in the library next morning. The solution
of course means the composite form of opera, but that
union lies outside the bounds of this particular opera: it
is to take place tomorrow morning at eleven precisely.

Prophetically adjusting time and deferring the solution, *Capriccio* closes with an apology for its own insufficiency as the Countess wonders whether there can be any conclusion which will not prove trivial and goes off to her supper. For all its rigorous artifice, the work is uncomfortably open-ended.

*Ariadne* at least presents an opera inside an opera, but *Capriccio* presents rehearsals, theoretical preliminaries, projects for the future, without ever bringing its intended work to birth. Actually it unmakes the union of arts it professes to long for. Its style and manner turn against music: Strauss insisted that he wanted a tough, dry, fugal, unmellifluous text, "no lyricism, no poetry, no outpouring of feeling," as he told Krauss in 1939, as if requiring a spare and penitential libretto in which words would not be erased by music. So discreet is the conversational musical setting that a reversal of operatic convention occurs, and song appears to be the banal medium in which the characters conduct their daily lives, while speech becomes the extraordinary medium reserved for spasms of poetic uplift. The recitation of the sonnet by the Count and Clairon is as startling as a song would be in a non-musical play. Flamand later sets it and the Countess sings it, but they trivialize it in doing so, enticing it back into innocuous tunefulness.

*Capriccio* reverses the operatic history it extols by making song aspire to the condition of speech. Despite its mannered unreality, it is, in this relapse from music into dialogue, apologetically realistic. Such a breakdown occurs at critical moments in later works—in Britten's *Peter Grimes* when Balstrode's prosaic instructions intrude on the lyrical derangement of Grimes's monologue, or in the same composer's *Death*

*in Venice* where Aschenbach's self-communing is rendered in pitched speech with piano accompaniment,
as it were an interpolated lieder recital punctuating the
opera. "Sprechgesang" explores the boundary between the painful honesty of speech and the lyrical
evasions of song which, as the Count says in *Capriccio*,
is word-murder. Schönberg's Moses stutters in prose,
his concern for truth to his vision denying him the glib
resources of song; Aron the publicist and propagandist
sings in garrulous dodecaphonic coloratura.

   The paradox of this realistic intimidation of opera is
that, while song declines into speech and musical convention founders, dramatic convention needs to be
reinforced. The personages of verismo opera are far
from being the humble, unspectacular characters of
realism. They are neither gods nor epic heroes, the
progeny of gods. Instead they belong to that genus
which is the modern equivalent of divinity, celebrities.
They are, for instance, the diva Tosca, the fatal woman
Turandot who attracts victims from all corners of the
earth, the courtesan Magda, the poets Rodolfo and
Andrea Chénier, the actresses Adriana Lecouvreur
and Clairon. Verismo is conceived in bad faith because, ashamed of the artifice of opera, it is driven to
rely on characters who are themselves artists and can
therefore be counted on to behave unrealistically in the
line of their trade: opera singers, actresses, clowns,
poets or painters, composers and their music-masters,
celebrated toreadors. For all their boast of verisimili-
tude, these works represent a new aestheticism. They
are art about art. Their characters sing not about love
or life or even politics but about the technical problems of their professions: Escamillo about his suave
mastery of the bullring, Cavaradossi about painting in

"Recondita armonia," Tosca about singing in "Vissi d'arte," Adriana about dramatic interpretation in "Io sono l'umile ancella," Andrea Chénier about poetic inspiration in "Come un bel dì di Maggio," Michonnet about stage management in "Ecco il monologo," La Roche and Tonio in his prologue elaborating programmes for a new realism in art, Strauss's Composer celebrating his gift in "Musik ist ein heilige Kunst."

The epic hero is the offspring of divinity: Siegmund of Wotan, Berlioz's Enée of Venus. The celebrity merely wears the garments of divinity and can easily slip out of them. Clairon leaving the rehearsal remarks that she and her colleagues are changing back from creatures of fable into figures who perform roles decreed by society, resuming their nonentity. The nonchalance with which she or the soprano and tenor in *Ariadne* assume the costumes and antics of the gods while professing not to believe in them catches the half-heartedness of verismo, which claims to despise illusion but cannot do without it.

The same evasion muddles the conclusion of the aesthetic debate in *Capriccio*. Although the Countess scorns triviality, the problem is solved by being trivialized. The Count's suggestion that mythological subjects should be abandoned, and that poet and composer should combine to dramatize the events of that afternoon, is a diplomatic maneuvre, not a seizure of imagination. Titillatingly combining indiscretion, as La Roche appreciates, and narcissism, it is, for all its pretensions to creative originality, a parody of the moment when Sachs in *Die Meistersinger,* having heard the prize-song, declares that a child has been born. The Countess has earlier referred to the accord between Olivier and Flamand as a blossoming tree growing tall from this moment. Her image declines into a mocking proverb when, after the Count's scheme is announced, Olivier and La Roche remark that a blind hen has laid an egg.

The pretense that the intrigues and attractions in the chateau can be made to constitute an allegory of the war between words and music is a cautionary way of trivializing the issues by personalizing them. Defused, the debate can proceed on gossipy "ad hominem" terms. The Countess is provided with a formula for extricating herself, since she can convert the aesthetic question into an erotic one and so be excused from having to decide. As an astute descendant of the Marschallin, she knows that the way to keep both lovers is to satisfy neither of them, and her teasing, coy device must stand for a resolution when it is in truth only an evasion. She consults her own reflection in the mirror and asks it to advise her—an apt image for the vanity into which the work retreats at its end. Throughout, it discusses theories and projects for an art-work of the future, to be accomplished in the future; then it wearily backdates the accomplishment and presents itself as that art-work. It is the prologue to *Ariadne* posing as the opera. The trouble with *Capriccio* is that it is merely capricious, flirting with its subject but not risking involvement, failing to keep its enticing promises. The coquette's wisdom is "Du fandest es süss, schwach zu sein," it is sweet to be weak.

Madeleine's self-admiration in the mirror is echoed by Strauss's self-quotations in the score. The orchestra refers to *Ariadne* and *Daphne* when those legends are proposed as possible operatic subjects, as if Strauss were mimicking the evasiveness of the drama by substituting the memory of past achievements for the new synthesis *Capriccio* talks about but fails to achieve.

Strauss's allusions to his past are an alibi. When Olivier and Flamand suggest Ariadne and Daphne as subjects for future exploration, Strauss can smugly remind them through the orchestra that the material belongs to him, and is exhausted. What the characters believe to be the future is already, for the composer, the past.

Reflections and echoes combine to make *Capriccio* a work of second-hand creativity. Even the string sextet which forms the prelude is identified at once as belonging to Flamand, as if a price tag were being affixed to it. Words and music reach the end of their long association not in the truce the Countess thinks she has arranged but in fatigued mutual surrender. Music declines into pastiche, words into parody. Though claiming to refer to Gluck's operatic reform which made way for the music-drama of the nineteenth century, *Capriccio* is defeatist, not revolutionary, a work in which the end of an artistic tradition dreams of the distant beginning.

Creativity at second hand makes the characters poetasters rather than artists, specialists in mimicry and pastiche. Values are, however, so far reversed that the most parasitic and slavish of them all is the only one possessed by a genuine creative excitement. This is the prompter, M. Taupe, who emerges from the dark theater where he has been abandoned after falling asleep on the job. His employers are too worldly to be artists, too preoccupied with social and sexual competition, but M. Taupe, as he tells the Major-Domo, is a transient in the world of reality. He belongs underground, invisibly commanding a magical kingdom: he is Alberich transmuted into an artist, enthroned in the depths of a Nibelheim which is not an industrial tyranny but a world-theater whose overseer directs its operations not with Alberich's whip-lashing fury but

in soporific whispers. He has the artist's gratification
of seeing his dream animated into truth before him,
and like the artist he is a hidden god who rules through
absence. In his region of shadows his own murmur
sends him to sleep, and it is then that he becomes a
sensation, for the actors are unable to continue and the
audience is awoken by the silence. He is vigilant so that
the world can sleep; when he sleeps, the world awakes
in fear. But even he is granted no god-like power of
initiation. He makes nothing, only remaking in his
guiding whispers what the poets have already written.
Yet his appearance in this work of formalistic symmetry is a dangerous accident, since it exposes and
diminishes even further the other characters who are
dependent on him.

The claims of literature have dwindled between
*Ariadne* and *Capriccio*. The Composer's omnipotence
as a creator and Zerbinetta's skill in improvizing altera-
tions are incompatible kinds of artistic power entangled together. A work of art is created as we watch, and
its tragicomic duplicity extends the Composer's brief
sentimental accord with Zerbinetta. But in *Capriccio*
there is only talk about interpreting works of art which
have already been created by others, and even this an-
cillary activity occurs elsewhere: the performance of
the sextet and the rehearsal take place in rooms adjoin-
ing the stage.

Strauss in earlier years had proclaimed the right of
music to take literature by force. At a performance of
*Pelléas et Mélisande* in Paris in 1907 he complained to
Romain Rolland that Debussy had failed to make
music master of the text, contenting himself with writing a servile and subdued musical commentary on
Maeterlinck's play. Hofmannsthal's hope in the early
critical essays discussed in this chapter had been the

same: music is to guarantee a romantic redemption for literature by finally effecting the conversion of drama, preoccupied with activity and exertion, into an introspective operatic equivalent of the novel. But music is for Hofmannsthal more a literary paradox than a sonic actuality. It is the "ditties of no tone" played for the spirit in Keats's poem, the lyrical silence of reverie, and in the event quite incompatible with the orchestral din fomented by Strauss. Hence the change which Elektra undergoes, from Hofmannsthal's incapable monologuist to Strauss's vixenish, invincible warrior-maiden. Hence the act of restitution, described in the previous chapter, which remakes *Die Frau ohne Schatten* as a novel. Hence the demoralization of *Ariadne,* which admits that the descent to myth is merely a ransacking of the costume wardrobe and that opera must be forever compromised by the extempory pretenses of the theater which Natasha Rostov and the romantic critics of Shakespeare found so lowering.

The arts derive no courage or consolation from the defensive merger Hofmannsthal proposes. Instead they are weakened, individually and collectively. By the time of *Capriccio,* music and literature are equally enfeebled. Song declines into speech, in accordance with the verismo misunderstanding of the nature of the operatic novel, while music retires to hum reticently behind the chatter of the salon. Words and music may quarrel about priority, but in truth they are both secondary. Their place has been usurped, as the final chapter will demonstrate, by the image. Although Strauss found *Pelléas* unacceptably timid, his own *Salome* is a case in which music besieges and obliterates a text. But Salome has outgrown both literature and music, and she leaves both behind to be canonized as an image by dance and painting.

# 5. Opera, Dance, and Painting

Depending on the conversion of one art into another and on the slippery interchangeability of languages, opera is particularly concerned with translation. Wilde's *Salomé* is doubly a victim of translation, forgotten by literature but preserved in music, and shuttled between languages. Wilde wrote it in French, intending it to be played by Sarah Bernhardt; Lord Alfred Douglas translated it into English; Strauss set a German version by Hedwig Lachmann. But there is a certain justice to the supercession of the play, for Salome is a character who repudiates literature, seeking alternatives first in music but then in arts which enshrine her as an image, self-absorbed, contentless, a profane icon. Having first relinquished speech for song, she abandons song for dance. At last even the dramatic energy of dance is renounced, and she settles into a passive pictorial object. This chapter will follow some of her metamorphoses to show how, having proposed itself as the central romantic art form, opera strangely discovers its own consummation beyond literature, in the symphonic poem.

Composition in a foreign language is the first defining oddity of Wilde's play, and it warns of the migrations which are to come. Wilde's choice of French places him in the interesting company of Beckford (in the sadistic fantasy *Vathek*) and Samuel Beckett, and in all three cases there is a correspondence between re-

nunciation of the native language and the artist's subject. The luridly ornamental orient of Beckford and
Wilde may seem remote from the penurious wastes of
Beckett, but they are alike in being adversary landscapes, contradictions of the actual. Beckford and
Wilde compose indulgent fantasies; Beckett corre-
sponds to them as their opposite, grim and self-deny-
ing where they are luxurious. All three write in French
because to do so is to enlist the aid of language against
nature. The fleshly paradises of Beckford and Wilde
are made out of linguistic excess, the purgatorial ash-
heaps of Beckett out of grudging linguistic reduction.
In a foreign language, style acquires the scientific
pitilessness Flaubert commends in the letter to Louise
Colet, annihilating not only emotion and morality but
the subject itself. Style becomes its own subject—in
Beckford and Wilde because words have become images, gaudily precious, in Beckett because only words,
though denuded of sense, remain in this vacant world.

Lachmann's translation into German makes a second metamorphosis, and has the virtue of rescuing
Wilde's play from itself, as Boïto felt Italian had res-
cued the befouled and victimized Falstaff. German
expunges the mannered refinement of the French and
gives to the heroine's utterances a guttural, visceral
avidity which is genuinely horrifying, where in
Wilde's phrasing she is merely peevish. Compare "J'ai
baisé ta bouche, Jokanaan" with "Ich habe deinen
Mund geküsst, Jokanaan." The one is pretty, social,
delicate, the other gross and lascivious, the very sound
imitating the slavering embrace. "Baisé" pecks,
"geküsst" positively slobbers. In French the summit of
the phrase is the noun, in German the verb. French
insists on the prize of which Salomé has taken posses-

sion, and on the mouth's conversion into a trophy (as in Flaubert's "Hérodias," in which the followers of Iaokanann rescue the severed head and carry it off towards the sea of Galilee: the head is now a precious but cumbrous object, and the disciples, its weary custodians, have to take turns in carrying it). German transfers attention to the verb and hence to the completion of an action. The cry of triumph is consequently erotic, not aesthetic.

From French to German, from Wilde's dramatic poem which is never permitted to become a drama to Strauss's blatant and exotic score, Salome is also vocally transformed. In Wilde she is petulant and wilful, with the impatience of adolescence which demands its satisfactions immediately (her childishness is also wittily registered by Flaubert: his Salomé struggles to remember the difficult name of the prophet whose head she has been instructed to demand). She is uncomfortably close to the spoiled and opinionated Cecily of *The Importance of Being Earnest,* and her monstrosity constantly threatens to regress into naughtiness. Strauss makes this captious adolescent a dramatic soprano, a creature of power and steely invincibility. The atmosphere of prurient trifling which diminishes Wilde's heroine gives way to fierce intensity and an equivocal heroism, for Salome is now engaged in combat not only with the court but with a brazen, convulsive orchestra.

Strauss's vocal requirements are perversely self-contradictory. His heroine is a pathological Isolde, and yet he claimed in later years that the ideal voice for the part was a silvery lyric soprano and coaxed Elisabeth Schumann to undertake it. For Jokanaan he demands the voice of a Wotan, yet condemns the god to sing mostly from the bottom of a cistern, while in the case of Herod (as with Aegisth in *Elektra*) he expects the voice of a heroic tenor to controvert itself by portraying an effeminate, babbling coward. Siegfried is assigned music fit for Mime. The opera is driven by contradictions such as these, which make it perverse rather than, like Wilde's play, salaciously teasing. The orchestral players are punished by Strauss's habit of writing parts at the extremes of the range of certain instruments. The dimensions of the work are awkwardly self-contradictory. It has breadth without length. As if following the aesthetics of Poe, it narrows the Wagnerian proliferation and prolixity into a single lyrical spasm; but it is lopsided, brief without being lean, since the orchestra has been extended and complicated. What it loses in time it gains in the amplitude of its choked sonic space. And yet the music is composed loudly so that it can be played softly—like Mendelssohn's fairy pieces, Strauss insisted.

Salome's transference to music is logical because, as Elektra tells Chrysothemis, the music comes from within her. Elektra however tortures feeling into verbal form, whereas in Salome musical desire obliterates reason and therefore speech. Salome is a creature of sense, and, as Kierkegaard argued, only music can give immediate, uncomplicated expression to the cravings of sensuality. Considering the various incarnations of the libertine, Kierkegaard disqualifies Byron's *Don Juan* because the libertine cannot be allowed to speak. Words are a medium of rational exchange incompatible with his burgeoning sensuous delight. Even in Mozart's opera, what Don Giovanni says (or rather sings) reveals less about him than does the overture, in which he has been disembodied into a natural and therefore symphonic force. As such he is an ancestor of Tristan and Isolde, who in the disturbed outer acts argue and analyze and rail with words, like characters in spoken drama, but in the central act are joined in the flux of music which washes away words.

As romantic opera subverts words, so it subverts morality. Sweeping away the evasions and apologies of language, remaking character as an image of will bereft of the alibis and rationalizations speech supplies, opera participates in that moral revolution which Shaw, defending Wagner against Nordau's charges of degeneracy, celebrates in "The Sanity of Art." Declaring Schopenhauer to be "a true pioneer in the forward march of the human spirit," Shaw turns the isolated case of Tristan and Isolde, who renounce the pretense of self-control and abandon themselves to desire, into a general law: "We can now, as soon as we are strong-minded enough, drop . . . the . . . subterfuges to which we cling because we are afraid to look life straight in the face and see in it, not the fulfilment of a moral law or of the deductions of reason, but the satisfaction of a passion in us of which we can give no rational account whatever."

This liberation of instinct connects Salome with what Kierkegaard saw as the exclusively musical character of Don Giovanni. His encyclopedic hunger becomes in her a greedy aestheticism, determined to lay hands on and own whatever she desires. Karl Böhm seemed to imply a connection between the early romantic hero of appetite unbridled and the late romantic heroine of appetite's iron, murderous whim when in 1965, at the Metropolitan Opera in New York, he conducted performances of *Salome* prefaced by Strauss's tone poem *Don Juan*.

The juxtaposition of opera and symphonic poem has another significance. Strauss's development of the Wagnerian form upsets Wagner's hoped-for equivalence between words and music. *Salome* and *Elektra* are fierce battles between verbal and musical drama, and the opposition between these formal elements is a symptom of psychological divisions within the heroines. Words represent enfeebled reason (the arid, disputatious rationality of the Jews, Herod's frantic argumentation in attempting to dissuade Salome), music the irresistible will of emotion. At the end Salome is incorporated into the orchestra, literally drowned by it, since, once her wish is granted, she sings with it rather than against it. At the last words fail Elektra, who at a similar moment of gratification collapses into the ocean of orchestral sound. These two works are a dead end of formal paradox in Strauss's development and in the history of opera, because words and music in challenging one another consume one another.

Expanded and refined into a virtuoso instrument, Strauss's orchestra boasts of having superseded words and therefore, by implication, opera. Strauss often joked about the mimetic skill of his symphonic poems, hinting that it should be possible to decipher from the score which of his Don Juan's victims was a red-head, and setting the writer of programme music tasks like composing a menu card or a glass of beer, which was to be so meticulously transcribed that the listener would be able to tell whether it was a Pilsener or a Kulmbacher. For Strauss the destiny of the music of the future was to render both literature and painting obsolete by taking over their work of realistic description and closing their archaic gap between form and

content. With jovial utopianism he looked forward to
the day when a musician would compose the silver on
a dinner table so as to differentiate spoons from forks,
and though he made this prophecy ironically he was
taken at his word by Ernest Newman, who in an essay
on programme music in 1905 praised Strauss's "pictorial faculty" as vastly superior to Wagner's and
commented that "things which would have seemed
impossible a hundred years ago are done with ease
today. . . . The representative power of music is
growing day by day."

Like Shaw's attack on Nordau, Newman's phrases
catch the evolutionary enthusiasm of the late
nineteenth century, the confidence that, as intellect extends its researches, objects however recalcitrant will
be abstracted into ideas and brute matter succumb to
the austere self-regard of mind. By turning objects into
music, Strauss is abolishing their dull, literal reality,
making them mental phenomena, knots of ingenious
complication to be disentangled.

This is a process parallel to that which was simultaneously taking place in painting. Abstraction in art is
the final triumph of mind in its long battle to enlighten
matter, since things—the mountains or fruit of
Cézanne, the haystacks of Monet—are seen being
transformed into representations, into ideas of themselves. A silver spoon is itself, a utensil, but Strauss in
setting it would have turned it into a notion of itself,
just as the melting cathedrals of Monet or the giants
decomposed into dots of Seurat are no longer things or
persons but are liquified (in Monet's case) or analyti-
cally reduced (in Seurat's) into an essence or a diagram
which stands for what they are, not (Hamlet's terms
recur) what they seem to be. The painting of the late

nineteenth century, like its programme music, enacts a dissolution of the world. The dream of Tristan and Isolde is being realized: the world is exposed as a shoddy facsimile and recomposed in the tranquil isolation of the mind. This is the contemplative course Pater recommends at the end of *The Renaissance,* the reflective dissipation of objects until they are "loosed into a group of impressions—colour, odour, texture—in the mind of the observer," the evanescence of things which language pretends are tough and durable into flickering images, until "the whole scope of observation is dwarfed into the narrow chamber of the individual mind."

That transformation may be overheard in *Salome.* Whenever a character mentions an object, the music at once finds an equivalent for it, a subjective correlative as it were, which renders the literary object redundant—the flower Salome promises to drop for Narraboth, the muslin veils through which she might look at him, the beating wings Herod imagines, the individual glints and lambencies of his jewels. Strauss's orchestra exerts itself to keep up with language, to translate each linguistic event into an impression, and it is this tireless activity of translation which makes music in Pater's account a symbol of consciousness, fluid and inconstant. "What is real in our life fines itself down" to a movement which outstrips analysis, since its impressions and sensations dissolve before they can be defined. As Arthur Symon says of the dancer in an essay which will be discussed later, "The picture lasts only long enough to have been there," like a thought in passage through the mind. Pater calls this meditative effort to apprehend fugitive impressions, to catch the tremors of our own senses and fix them briefly as ideas,

"that continual vanishing away, that strange, per-
petual weaving and unweaving of ourselves," and the
sinuousness of the phrase suggests something of the
elasticity of Strauss's score, forever assuming new
shapes, relentlessly remaking itself.

Although Ernest Newman was later to become the
biographer of Wagner and an increasingly harsh critic
of Strauss, in the 1905 essay on programme music he
points to the symphonic poem as the rightful successor
to Wagnerian music–drama, for the paradoxical reason
that it has engorged and therefore eliminated words:
"This form, I contend, is the only form that can be
deduced logically from Wagner's own aesthetic
theory," although it inverts and undoes that theory.
Opera remains residually materialist because words
are a "non–emotional substance." The symphonic
poem declares the victory of mind over intractable
matter because it makes everything poetic, omitting all
prosaic occasion and labored justification.

Interestingly, Newman chooses to make his point
by way of a literary analogy. He interprets Browning's
epic of mental detection, *The Ring and the Book* (already
noticed in the first chapter as epic democratized), as a
fable in which artistic creation proceeds to liberate itself from the support of form and material detail.
Browning's image refers to the fashioning of a gold
ring by a workman who "in order to make his material
workable . . . has to blend an alloy with the gold: but
when the circle is complete he drives out the alloy with
a spirt of acid, leaving the pure metal only. That is the
symphonic poem; the opera is the ring with the alloy
left in it." Newman's use of Browning's poem is an
ironic coincidence, since *The Ring and the Book* is contemporary with Wagner's *Ring,* and these vast works

share not only a central metaphor but a common
artistic procedure. Both were written backwards.
Browning discovers the book containing details of the
Renaissance crime and from it makes the ring by a ret-
rospective exercise of imagination, reanimating the
past. Wagner's tetralogy describes two arches in time.
Philosophically it extends forwards, from the revolutionary optimism of 1848, diagnosing the contradictions of an economic regime and nominating Siegfried as its fearless opponent, to the fatalism of
Schopenhauer and Brünnhilde's recognition that redemption comes from self-sacrificing love, not from a
change in political and economic arrangements. But
dramatically it was conceived backwards, beginning
with Siegfried's death and gradually unravelling behind this all the anterior evidence necessary to account
for the significance of that death. Browning's ring is
art, achieved by purifying life of its evasions and in-
completeness. Wagner's ring is a beguiling parody of
art, an object craved for the power it bestows, the
enemy of life. Newman has used Wagner's own talisman against him. Formally, the ring implies the work's
circularity, mythically doubling back to its beginning,
and Wagner's holistic merger of the arts, but these
senses too Newman makes it disown. Abandoning
the syncretism of Wagner's theory, he encourages
music to expel from the alliance the other arts which,
in Pater's phrase, are parasitically aspiring to its condition. Newman continued to think the theater a
hampering influence on Strauss. Reviewing *Der Rosen-
kavalier* in Birmingham in 1913, he took the opportunity to wish that Strauss would renounce opera
"and concentrate upon some purely orchestral work
that would call out all the best that is in him."

Salome has three weapons against words. The first is music, which Newman incites to suppress words. The others are dance and painting. When Salome dances, she ceases to be a character and becomes an image, and opera turns simultaneously into a symphonic poem, into a ballet, and into a painting.

The dancer is one of romanticism's notions of itself in its terminal stages, because her art represents a perfect, and vacuous, fusion of form and content. She is an inextricable compound of subject and object, like Newman's gold circle, since the medium of her art is her own body. She needs simply to be herself beautifully, without pretending to a meaning. Her body thinks for her. Salome is the last in a tradition of romantic acrobats, virtuosi who play upon the instruments of themselves, of whom the first is perhaps Rameau's nephew in Diderot's dialogue, a dangerously capricious man of feeling who twists his body into painful contortions in the hope of penitentially loosening nature into the suppleness of art. As the nephew plays a soundless symphony on instruments which sprout invisibly from his arms and legs, so the dancers of the 1890s make silent music, which Keats had declared to be sweeter than the melodies apprehended by "the sensual ear." The dancer pipes "to the spirit ditties of no tone"; as Arthur Symons put it in a poem of 1895, "To a Dancer,"

> Her body's melody,
> In silent waves of wandering sound,
> Thrills to the sense of all around.

Another poem by Symons describes the performance of La Mélinite at the Moulin Rouge. Like Salome or Pater's Gioconda, she has "about her a de-

praved virginity," and her dance (performed to
Olivier Metra's "Waltz of the Roses") is not intended
for the pleasure of others but is coolly self-referring,
addressed to her reflection in a mirror. Hence in dancing she transforms herself into an image:

> Before the mirror's dance of shadows
> She dances in a dream,
> And she and they together seem
> A dance of shadows,
> Alike the shadows of a dream.

Dancing "for her own delight" and ambiguously smil-
ing at her reflection, she has the narcissism which
Wilde considered to be the last refinement of beauty
and the immaculate emptiness praised by Lord Henry
in *The Picture of Dorian Gray:* "People say sometimes
that Beauty is only superficial. That may be so. But at
least it is not so superficial as Thought is." The dancer
marks the final deathly abstraction of the image, self-
made and self-admiring, moving motionlessly to silent music.

In 1898 Symons contributed a study of "Ballet, Pantomime, and Poetic Drama" to the first number of *The
Dome,* and here he returns to the aesthetic significance
of the dancer and the concurrent transformation of
opera, by the suppression of both music and text, into
image. The three forms he studies have in common an
enmity towards language. Ballet and pantomime do
without it, since they enable us to overhear the body
thinking, and they begin and end "before words have
formed themselves, in a deeper consciousness than that
of speech." Even poetic drama subdues language and
action to the creation of motionless tableaux. In the
performance of *Parsifal* at Bayreuth in 1897 which Sy-

mons describes, music absorbs and obliterates the verbal drama. But more than this, the destiny of music is now conceived to be transformation into its silent opposite in the manufacture of "pictures, abstract pictures; . . . even the music, as one watches the stage, seems to subordinate itself to the visible picture there." Ballet, pantomime, and the Wagnerian poetic drama agree in celebrating the conversion of drama into picture.

The pictorial *Parsifal* of Symons was renewed at Bayreuth in 1951 in the production by Wieland Wagner, whose aesthetic apprenticeship had been as a painter. Wieland's hieratic stillness and abstract evacuation of scenery, though considered dangerously radical, in fact scrupulously adhere to the tradition of the 1890s. *Parsifal* volunteers for such pictorial treatment because its interludes proclaim it as a picture which moves. The interfusion of space and time which Gurnemanz celebrates has been mentioned in the previous chapter as a justification for the novelistic interpretation of opera, since it is a case of Forster's expansion. Here, in the context of Symons's remarks, it is also a justification for the pictorial interpretation of the form.

The first section of Symons's essay treats "The World as Ballet," and argues that dance delights the abstract thinker as it offends the moralist because its material is "animal life, having its own way passionately," the ecstatic madness which the ancients knew to be sacred and which consumes Salome and Elektra. Dance contributes to that revolutionary unshackling of instinct which Shaw hails in Schopenhauer. But as Tristan and Isolde choose to turn their instinctual freedom into a chaste mental separateness, disdaining mere physical consummation, so the dancer is the more hedonistically liberated for being coolly abstract, representing an idea, not merely flaunting her body. Dance is a mimicry of instinct doubly abstracted, since it not only idealizes acts and makes pictures of them, "it is more than a beautiful reflection, it has in it life itself, as it shadows life; and it is farther from life than a picture." It is both the spontaneous delight of instinct and the stylization of that natural grace into shadowplay, "more natural than nature, more artificial than art."

These contradictions recall the prefatory epigrams in *Dorian Gray.* So far as form is concerned, Wilde nominates the musician as the type of the artist. As concerns feeling, the actor is the exemplar. Both are profoundly superficial, the musician delighting in form emptied of content, the actor specializing in the simulation of feeling, in the formalistic pretense of content. Becoming as she does a type of the artist in this period, Salome inevitably turns into a musician and an actress, a detached performer.

The dancer is an incitement to hedonism—not Herod's lust, but the abstracted relishing of sensation described by Pater. Symons says that dancers "sum up in themselves the appeal of everything in the world that is passing, and coloured, and to be enjoyed: everything that bids us to take no thought for the morrow, and dissolve the will into slumber, and give way luxuriously to the delightful present." The luxurious dissolution of the present points to the Schopenhauerian philosophy of Tristan and Isolde; but they drown the will by singing it to sleep, whereas Symons now recasts them as dancers tiring the will in hypnotic movement. He concludes by describing the dance as an attempt "to do the impossible—to create life." Ballet

has become the realm of Frankenstein, for as the world
is not substantial but "a masque of shadows," the artist, Symons argues, is driven by a desire to both en-
force its illusoriness and evade it by creating something "of at least the same shadowy reality as that
about us." The ballet offers the form in which life can
be fabricated, since in it the static picture is animated,
and its every motion is "pure symbol." The modern
Prometheus snatching the secret of life from the gods
is no longer a scientist (as in Mary Shelley's novel) but
a choreographer.

Given this idealization of the dancer, whose art dis-
penses with the dramatist's intrusive use of words, it is
ironically apt that Strauss should have composed
Salome's dance last, after the rest of the score had been
completed. He seems almost to have recognized that
dance is a separate extension of her, a new form in
which she has ceased to be a dramatic character; and
the dance has indeed acquired its own separate existence as a tone-poem, in the absence of a dancer.

Words are silenced by dance again in *Elektra*—the
heroine's last cry to Chrysothemis is that people as
overjoyed as they are should be silent, and dance.
Elektra's dance is not erotically persuasive but an obsessive tarantella like that of Ibsen's Nora, a convulsive
dance of death. After her initial monologue Elektra
rehearses her dance of triumph as a private fantasy,
shamingly interrupted by Chrysothemis; when the
executions are accomplished she returns to it as a public ceremonial, and it exhausts and destroys her. Dance
began in the worship of what Symons calls "the disturbing deities," the gods who delight in the explosive
excess of natural force, and in Elektra's case the Viennese waltz becomes a reincarnation of that dangerous

cult. Hofmannsthal has turned the implacable fate of Greek tragedy into an image of neurotic compulsion. It is not the gods who torment his characters but the characters who create their own mental prisons by brooding on their sickness. Tragedy, no longer a religious system, has contracted into a state of mind, and Elektra's dance is the Freudian patient's surrender to mania. Nietzsche saw the origins of tragedy in music and dance, and in Elektra's frenzy tragedy incorporates the psychiatry of Freud and a demented version of the waltz as a way back to those origins.

Romantic art in its decadence exchanges its earlier religion of nature for an aesthetic religion of the unnatural. The icon, sacred and ministering to religious knowledge, is supplanted by the image, profane and self-absorbed, disdaining reference to anything beyond itself. The artist has become a magus and a high priest, but the religion he serves is a parodic one. Salome flourishes in this atmosphere of perverted spirituality, where religious ardor merges into sexual desire and all the senses are synesthetically exploited and deranged. Keats said that the imagination of the romantic poet resembled Adam's dream of Eve—he awoke and found it truth. The imaginations of the later, decadent romantics resemble Salome's dream of Jokanaan—it does not come true with the happy naturalness of Adam's; she wills it into truth at the cost of his life.

The formula of "The Ballad of Reading Gaol," that "all men kill the thing they love," is not so much an expression of dismay as a positive injunction. Destroying is preserving. The head when the executioner lifts it from the cistern has become an art-object, a sacred trophy, and Salome's feelings towards it in the final scene are repulsive not because they are erotic but because they are aesthetic. She gloats over it as her creation and possession. Her defense lies in the aesthetic morality declaimed in the preface to *Dorian Gray:* like the artist she abolishes ethical sympathies and is safe from the accusation of morbidity because the artist has the right to "express anything." She glories in the uselessness of art. Though free to do as she wishes with the head, she has no use for it once it has been detached from the body she desired: it now exists simply to be admired.

Both the play and the opera are treasuries of images—precious objects, jewels, garments, tropical fruits, and exotic creatures. Wilde names them and Strauss conjures them up in sound. The score has a rank luxuriance which suggests the painters of the Wiener Sezession or Art Nouveau. As in Art Nouveau lines coil, twine, and proliferate in a jungle of decorative vegetation, so Strauss's music has an uncanny biological liveliness, a readiness to describe and envelop any incident, however unmusical, mentioned by Wilde. It has a grotesque excess of refinement, and though dionysiacally noisy, it wilts (like Beardsley's limp Siegfried) under the strain of its disproportionate strength. The first bars of the opera, in which coiling woodwinds describe the humid atmosphere of the night, are virtually a musical transcription of the twisted, lithe, involuted lines of Art Nouveau, creepers which elegantly strangle any object they are trained over.

Painter as well as dancer, Salome herself approaches seduction pictorially. In her three imploring addresses to Jokanaan she turns his body into a series of landscapes. At first his torso is blanched, frosty, and pure, made of lilies and snow: its painter might have been Odilon Redon. Then his hair hangs in thick clusters of grapes, or resembles cedars where lions and robbers lurk, as heavily sensuous as a picture by Klimt. Finally his mouth blazes scarlet like a pomegranate, coral branch, or azalea: this has the jewelled glare of the Byzantine fantasies of Moreau. Having created these pictures, Salome at once asserts her aesthetic prerogative and destroys them. As the picture records the degeneration of Dorian Gray, so she describes Jokanaan's flesh turning leprous and viperish and his hair becoming dusty and filthy, a crown of nettles and a nest of serpents.

Her triple appeal to the flesh, hair, and mouth of Jokanaan is balanced towards the end of the work by Herod's desperate entreaties, in which he too argues pictorially, offering her, instead of the head she covets, peacocks, priceless jewels, the mantle of the high priest, and the veil of the temple, wooing her with art-objects. She has already specified, with fastidious aestheticism, that she wishes the head in a silver charger. For all their differences, there is an aesthetic conspiracy between Herod and Salome, who are united in opposition to Herodias, the dull enemy of imagination for whom the moon is merely the moon, and nothing more, whereas her husband and daughter know it to be a disturbing metaphor.

Herod is a harmless aesthete, locking up his jewels out of his wife's reach. The horror of Salome is that she collects not gems but living creatures and is prepared to kill to add to her collection. In this she is again a figure of the artist, for style in decadent art asphyxiates its subject, and Salome's self-justification is the same as that of a spiritual descendant of hers, Jean Genet, who has argued that the application of style redeems the most brutal and sordid subject matter. Genet has declared that if his novels arouse the reader sexually "they're badly written, because the poetic emotion should be so strong that no reader is moved sexually. Insofar as my books are pornographic, I don't reject them. I simply say I lacked grace." The grace of form is meant to atone for and abolish the lubricity of content. The process is the same as that of abstraction, mentioned earlier, whereby in painting or in the symphonic poem brutish solid objects are dissolved and dissipated by the ingenuity of style. Wilde anticipates Genet in the preface to *Dorian Gray,* which insists that "those who find ugly meanings in beautiful things are corrupt without being charming. This is a fault," and it is a fault which Herod perhaps shares. An imprecise critic, he misunderstands Salome and calls her a monster because she has fallen from the grace of aesthetic detachment into pornography. She develops a lecherous craving for a work of art and slips from icy composure into the mess of human emotion, which Herod cannot forgive.

Wilde's play begins from painting. Its occasion was the passage in Huysmans' *A Rebours* in which des Esseintes reflects on the two versions of Salome by Moreau. From the start the idea of Salome is subject to metamorphosis: Wilde is developing a literary description of pictures which are themselves compounds of the other arts, for Huysmans argues that Moreau's images are disconcerting because of their ambiguous eclecticism, crossing the frontiers of painting to borrow hints and evocations from the writer, brilliance from the enamellist, and delicacy from the lapidarist or etcher. Huysmans also points out that Moreau's conception of Salome is gratuitous, a puzzling expan-

sion of the laconic gospel source. Her reappearance in
art originates both in transmissions from one artistic
medium to another and in disturbingly novel interpretation, so that the migration to opera is simply another
in an infinite series of metamorphoses. She is as ubiquitous as Auden's Queen of the Night.

The gospel writers are accused of possessing a quite
inadequate idea of her. In Matthew's version she is
simply a go-between who carries the head she has
earned back to her mother, and Herodias remains the
commanding character in Flaubert's tale and Mal-
larmé's poem. Nor have the painters of the classical
tradition done her justice. Their interests are fleshly
rather than morbidly spiritual, so that Cranach, in a
picture in the Museu de Arte Antiga in Lisbon, swathes
her in furs and gives her a numb, impassive expression
of boredom, while Rubens (the case Huysmans mentions) makes her the gross wife of a Flemish butcher.
Only when painting outgrows its attachment to substance and solidity and moves inwards, seeking to represent the unpaintable but musical world of thought
and desire, does Salome become its patroness, since she
too declares the triumph of image over material fact:
she makes an image of herself when she dances and an
image of Jokanaan's head when she has it severed. Nor
are the writers allowed any claim on her. Huysmans
charges that they have always failed to understand
"l'inquiétante exaltation de la danseuse, la grandeur
raffinée de l'assassine." The implication is that Salome
belongs in the wordless realm of dance described by
Symons, where her body constitutes both form and
content, and in music, which can express her desire
without the obligation to analyze or justify it which
literature incurs.

Moreau's conception far exceeds the data supplied

by the New Testament, as Huysmans acknowledges.
Salome is recreated in fantastic, subversive surmise,
and in metamorphoses not only from one artistic
medium to another but across the breadth of space and
down the length of time. In space, Moreau abstracts
her, as Huysmans points out, from Biblical tradition
and removes her to the theogonies of the Far East,
placing in her hand a lotus blossom, the scepter of Isis
and the sacred flower of Egypt and India, a phallic
emblem or the token of a sacrifice of virginity. He
removes her from time in declining to give precise
indication of race, country, or epoch, "en mettant sa
Salomé au milieu de cet extraordinaire palais, d'un
style confus et grandiose," making her inhabit indeed a
museum (the institution for the abolition of history
discussed in the first chapter of this book, and in the
commentary on Hofmannsthal's triad of Homer,
Shakespeare, and Rembrandt) comprising the art of all
times and places. Salome's initial translation into an
image is followed by this translation into a myth,
which, as with Auden's Queen of the Night, univer-
salizes her. Now an oriental deity, she has taken on the
ubiquity of Pater's Mona Lisa, another restlessly migratory image who has moved from painting to literature, from one sex to another, and who wanders
through various incarnations: "She has been dead
many times, and learned the secrets of the grave; and
has been a diver in deep seas . . . ; and trafficked for
strange webs with Eastern merchants; and, as Leda,
was the mother of Helen of Troy, and, as Saint Anne,
the mother of Mary."

Involving Salome in the primordial religious obser-
vances of India, in Hindu allegories of life, or in the
sepulchral ceremonies of ancient Egypt, Huysmans

makes her one of the undying gods of nature ritual. This too anticipates her eventual translation to music, since it places her in the company of those romance heroes who (as Jessie L. Weston argued in *From Ritual to Romance,* the anthropological study which underlies Eliot's *The Waste Land*) are rediscovered by Wagner and made to act out again, in modern psychological conflict, their ancient myths of quest and initiation. Salome the "énigmatique déesse" becomes a fellow-sufferer with Wagner's ailing fisher-king Amfortas: Huysmans recalls the solemn practices of embalmment, the careful extraction of the dead woman's insides while the body is laid on a slab of jasper. Like the sacrificed and dismembered god, and like her own victim Jokanaan, she is destroyed to be preserved. Once eviscerated, her nails and teeth are gilded and the body is anointed with oils and spices. She is granted the immortality of the image.

Another of Huysman's surmises appears to move her towards Kundry, caught between the undefiled Parsifal and the demonic spell of Klingsor as Salome is between the prophet and her lecherous stepfather. The lotus, Huysmans ventures, perhaps signifies "un échange de sang, une plaie impure sollicitée, offerte sous la condition expresse d'un meurtre," which hints at the venereal wounding of Amfortas and Kundry's hope of achieving redemption through the corruption of Parsifal. Klingsor mentions that one of Kundry's incarnations in her career of many deaths was as Herodias.

Huysmans treats Moreau's Salome as a creation of ethnological research, shared between the cults and superstitions which lie at the source of all religions. But even this anthropological interpretation releases her into music, for the primary universal language whose existence Lévi-Strauss postulates, in which the Babel of diverse tongues and warring theologies return to their original unity, is music, the international idiom. Moreau is amassing evidence for Salome's eventual migration to music in decoding the primary universal language and establishing the basic identity of religions, "remontant aux sources ethnographiques, aux origines de mythologies dont il comparait et démêlait les sanglantes énigmes; réunissant, fondant en une seule les légendes issues de l'Extrême-Orient et métamorphosées par les croyances des autres peuples." As Siegfried or Parsifal are, in Jessie Weston's view, nature gods who have made the long journey from ritual to romance and turned into chivalric heroes, so Salome is a cult figure who at this late stage has become an image. Anthropology canonizes her, making her ironically a more spiritual character than the baptist, who is a propagandist for one religion while she is a force in them all. The study of comparative religion in which Huysmans sees the origins of Salome is incidental comedy in Wilde's play and Strauss's setting, with the polyphonic squabbling of the Jews (like the obstreperous petitioners at the Marschallin's reception in *Der Rosenkavalier*) opposed to the grave certainty of the Nazarenes, and Jokanaan's cryptically fanatical utterances from under the floor punctuating Herod's nervous efforts to placate those of all persuasions above ground.

Deification confirms Salome's translation from nature to art. When she removes her clothes to dance she reveals not flesh but jewels. Her body is turning into a graven image: "Elle n'est plus vêtue que de matières orfévries et de minéraux lucides," notes Huysmans.

Where there is a glimpse of exposed flesh between the gorgerin and the girdle, he remarks that her navel resembles "un cachet gravé d'onyx, aux tons laiteux, aux teintes de rose d'ongle."

Hardening into an image, Salome becomes the property of the painters. Music and the anthropological speculations of Huysmans have been her unmaking as a character. She has first made the transition, described in the Hofmannsthal essays discussed in the previous chapter, from drama to novel: she expands, that is, from a person into a destiny, in the terms of Hofmannsthal's Balzac, from a product into a process. But the continuous and infinitely various nature of the process means that she can no longer pretend to possess a single, definable character. Instead she becomes a compendium of eternal but oddly assorted human traits, as encyclopedic as Kundry, who has worked her way through a variety of names during her agonizing pilgrimage down the centuries, or the Lulu of Wedekind and Berg, who sheds names and identities as effortlessly as if they were dresses. Embodiment in a character can never be, for such creatures, more than a temporary impersonation, since it is their episodic destiny to comprise all human types, perambulating through all times and places. Hence they become, like Pater's Mona Lisa or Moreau's Salome in Huysmans' analysis or Lulu (who is enshrined in Alwa's opera, Hugenberg's poetry, and the paintings of Schwarz and Geschwitz), exhibits in a museum, for the museum is the institution which equalizes all periods of time and juxtaposes the furthest reaches of space. Salome in particular unfurls into an array of images, hung in a gallery which is a shadowy mental theater where each spectator can find the fantasy which suits him.

As a model, she has a prostitute's obliging adaptiveness, ready to comply with the most recondite requests. For Wilde she can be a tiresome, petulantly epigrammatic Cecily; for Strauss, a raging, passionate Isolde; for Moreau, a bejewelled oriental priestess. This mythic versatility is a quality she shares with the Shakespearean characters of the second chapter: the obsessional Hamlet of Berlioz, the Tuscan Falstaff of Verdi. And as Falstaff generates wit in others, so Salome has no character in herself but derives a new persona from the use to which each new client puts her. If the gods of *Ariadne auf Naxos* have turned Olympus, as was argued in the preceding chapter, into a theatrical outfitter's establishment, Salome is a goddess who turns it into a brothel of cerebral fantasy.

Each new version of her is the artist's self-portrait. Beardsley made a drawing of the final scene of the play which appeared in *The Studio,* no. 1 in April, 1893, and the following year provided a set of mockingly frivolous, dandified illustrations for the first edition of the translation by Lord Alfred Douglas. The 1893 drawing reduces Wilde's lavish literary color-scheme to a stark black and white in a design which is prickly and predatory. The vegetative growths of Art Nouveau swarm, writhe, and bubble over the page, but in this case they are thorny rather than tropical. Salome is a Medusa with hair like seaweed and hirsute slippers. Her face is rough and masculine, Jokanaan's weak and feminine; her lips curl lasciviously, his have a girlish pout. This is an entomological Salome: she is a praying mantis on her wedding night.

As she evolves, Salome conducts a sour diagnosis of romantic emotion, exposing the disease and sexual confusion which its sentimental fictions palliate. She

11. Beardsley's Salomé of 1893: a praying mantis.

makes possible, for instance, a new and cruelly ironic interpretation of Isolde, for whom, as for Auden's Queen of the Night, Freud has added new synonyms to the thesaurus. For Salvador Dali Isolde is, like Beardsley's ravenous insect of 1893, a praying mantis, a cannibal denying Tristan physical consummation so as to incite him to the hysterical subterfuge of sublimation which prompts his nervous collapse. Their relationship is now one of moral torture. In 1940 Dali drew Isolde as a plumply fecund insect wearing down into distraught emaciation a kneeling, begging Tristan, his ribs protruding and his sex mournfully limp.

Munch's version of Eva Muddoci as Salome also turns romantic ecstasy into sexual war. The women of Munch are rapacious Isoldes, creatures of undifferentiated fertility who seek to absorb and engulf men. For their male victims, as for the deranged Tristan, sex betokens a sacrifice of identity indistinguishable from death. The "Liebesnacht" becomes in Munch's version a joylessly neurotic coupling. The woman, whose hair spreads through the design like rampant vegetation, smiles in the pleasure of possession; the man's head, her trophy, is wasting as we watch into a skull. Similarly, Klimt's "Judith (II) Salome" (1909) is a ravaged neurotic whose hands have thinned to claws which clutch the severed head. Though she is fashionably over-dressed, her breasts are bare and sharp as weapons. She is a ravaged, middle-aged society lady, closer to Herodias than to her daughter, or perhaps most like Hofmannsthal's menopausal Klytemnestra bedecked with jewels to ward off evil spirits. Her body is a collage of decorative fabrics, patched together in conflicting areas of design which threaten to fly apart in dissociation.

Salome has, however, another, a comic, history which is inaugurated by Beardsley's 1894 series. Her graduation to myth gives her the freedom of both tragedy and comedy: in nonchalant alternation, she can be either monstrous or frivolous, as Don Giovanni can oscillate between the tragic role of heaven's nobly consistent opponent and the comic role of encyclopedic philanderer. In 1894, Salome has retreated from the risks of lust and possession and learned the virtue and safety of self-love. Beardsley's listless decorativeness disowns emotion. She sits absorbed at her toilette, the works of de Sade and Zola conspicuous on her dressing table, suffering the action of the play only because of its opportunities for costume changes: a peacock skirt, a black cape of jagged tiers, and transparent knickers for the stomach dance. Like the gods mentioned earlier, she is not Salome, but someone half-heartedly playing the role. In the tailpiece she is laid to rest by a satyr and a foetus in Japanese attire inside the coffin of a powder box, a recollection perhaps of the embalming described by Huysmans. Cosmetics, fashion, and ornament have enabled her, as they do Beardsley's Belinda in his designs for "The Rape of the Lock," to suppress nature and remake herself as empty art, an image devoted to reverent self-admiration.

The nomadic course Salome follows, from literature to music, from opera to the symphonic poem, moving at last to dance and painting, is a final illustration of two of the preoccupations of this book. One is the need of certain literary characters to be released from literature. The other, corresponding to it, is the querulous, dissatisfied, ironic, romantic way with artistic form.

Character is for the romantics not a uniform of foi-

12. Alastair's Salomé of 1927: a mannequin.

bles and external traits in which a person is encased
before he enters the world. It is not reducible to an
assembly of characteristics. Art before the nineteenth
century envisages character as we see other people: as
objects. Romanticism envisages character as we see
ourselves: as subjects, elusive and indefinable. Character is not something with which we are equipped but
something we spend a lifetime's experience making
for ourselves, and that task is never completed. The
difference between the two notions is, as has been argued throughout this book, that between drama and
novel, and music confirms the novelistic view of
character. The overture to *Don Giovanni* or the prelude
to *Tristan* or Salome's dance do not refer to those
characters as dramatic entities, the kind of individuals
whose actions are recorded by history or adjudged by
law, but as forces or spirits, impulsive, impersonal because more than personal, and endlessly recurrent.

Being a principle of growth, character resists restric-
tion to any single embodiment: hence recurrences like
the transformation of Prospero into Berlioz's discipli-
narian conductor, or of the bemused characters of *Die
Zauberflöte* into Goethe's philosophical seekers, Hofmannsthal's infertile phantoms, or Auden's academic
refugees. Artists like these volunteer to grant characters immured in drama a resurrection in the novel.
Proposing a new ending for *Robinson Crusoe,* George
Moore in *Avowals* justifies the intrusion musically, offering to do "for Defoe what Wagner did for Gluck
and what Liszt did for many writers. Why should the
arrangements of masterpieces be limited to music?"

The rescue, in the case of the continuations of *Die
Zauberflöte,* involves freeing the characters from the
toils of music, but elsewhere in this study it is music

which promises liberation to characters chafing
against the restrictions of literature. Kierkegaard insists that the libertine is traduced by literature, which
condemns him to articulacy and intelligibility: his
rightful incarnation is in Mozart's score, not Byron's
garrulous verse. Salome also finds in music a medium
of sensuous immediacy which grants her wishes without the apologetic preliminaries of language. It is in the
orchestra, during the meditative passage between
Jokanaan's indignant return to the cistern and Herod's
entrance, that she has the inspiration of demanding the
head. The score voices it as a wish long before words
can bludgeon Herod into admitting it as an actuality.
So completely is Wilde's text consumed by music that
symphonic passages like this interlude of frustration
and the combined languor and ferocity of the dance,
rather than any of her words, reveal the secret of
Salome. Beyond this, her move to dance and painting
marks her final transformation from a character into an
image. For music she is still an emotional subject,
whose eerie virginity and panic of attraction and loath-
ing are characterized by the timbres of Strauss's orchestra; but she longs to renounce emotion and take on
the invulnerable self-satisfied finality of an aesthetic
object, which dance and painting permit her to do.

In the romantic understanding, Falstaff's is a similar
case. He is, in the first place, misrepresented by drama.
Tolstoy had a pious objection to drama similar to
Natasha's revulsion from opera. In drama a character
can have no existence beyond what he says, since there
is no novelist to ponder his motives or to overhear his
communion with himself, and for Tolstoy Falstaff
takes this condition of drama to its final audacious
absurdity. He is Shakespeare's truest character because

he is so brazenly a liar and a braggart. He does on principle what all the other characters are humiliatingly compelled to do by their existence in a drama: he struttingly advertises himself. He exposes the emptiness of the dramatic form, but in doing so unremorsefully atones for it. In this sense, although Tolstoy would not have assented, music is Falstaff's defense, turning his lies into blameless acts of imagination. Music supplies him with vocal qualities of vitality, juvenility, and inventiveness which belie his ponderous bulk, and it novelistically saves him from that state of self-publicizing self-creation which Tolstoy found so offensive in the character of drama.

But there is a second, more radical objection to Falstaff. Tolstoy pities him for being imprisoned in the mendacity of drama; George Moore pities him for being imprisoned in literature. In *Avowals* he describes an attempt to convince Beerbohm Tree of the character's unsatisfactoriness. To Moore, Falstaff is "too heavily intellectualized to be acted," a character exhausted by his creator's exploitations and driven into a dead-end of verbiage. Increasingly Falstaff is left with nothing to do but prose on, delivering lectures on honor and associated subjects as if writing daily columns in a newspaper, driven to the manufacture of opinions. Moore's criticism is as twisted as Tolstoy's, but its very perversity illuminates the relation between Shakespeare's plays and the opera. While Falstaff merely talks, his versions of himself may seem spurious, his business affairs and political ambitions shabby or preposterous, since he needs constantly to prop up his fictions and intimidate rational objection. Once he begins to sing, he is changed: buoyed up by Verdi's melodic generosity, he becomes the spirit of revelry

and jovial disorder which, in speech, he can only pretend to be. The argumentative tactics of Tolstoy and
Moore are revived by Auden, who declares that
Falstaff merely passes through Shakespearean drama
on the way to his definitive incarnation in opera buffa.

Evasions of literature like these recapitulate the
larger romantic disquiet about form, to which opera,
being a problematic union of the arts, is central. Sus-
pecting that any form is a hampering externality, a
letter which cages the spirit, a trapping or suit such as
Hamlet derides, romanticism ironically inverts forms
or hybridizes them or synoptically gathers them together in the hope of creating a confusion which
evades form altogether. It is not only that, in the
romantic period, the arts aspire to the condition of
music. In its turn music aspires to the conditions of
literature and even (in Newman's account of the symphonic poem) of painting. Each art, it might be said,
aspires to any condition but its own, just as characters
like Hamlet or Falstaff, whose whole existence is in
linguistic fabrication, in punning, riddling, and the
analysis of metaphors, long to rid themselves of the
self-consciousness of language in the inarticulate peace
of music.

This book has found such paradoxical combinations
and contradictions of forms everywhere. Wagner designs the *Ring* as a history of literary form, but its
sequence runs backwards, suggesting that the development of literature is entropic and mythically in-
consequential, beginning at the end and ending at the
beginning. Shakespeare's plays are narrowed into lyrical poems, their boisterous society scaled down to a
sentimental, symphonic monologue. Drama is turned
into its opposite, the novel, as music invades it. The

operatic union of the arts is hardly the industrial merger it seems, for it involves a virtual extinction of each art in turn. Wagner renders the orchestra invisible and wishes he could do the same to the theater. (The impenetrable gloom favored by modern lighting technicians in productions of his operas has posthumously granted him his wish.) Hofmannsthal longs to make literature musical, but the music, he at last realizes, must be silent and psychological. Opera itself, having undertaken to annex literature, expels it again, convinced (as this chapter has shown) that its consummation lies in the symphonic poem or even, in Symons's account of *Parsifal,* beyond music in the silent and wordless realm of imagery.

Opera does more than suffer conflicts like these: it foments them. Its genius lies in the potentiality for an enriching contradiction between its elements. Rather than a sedate marriage between text and music, it proposes a relationship of unremitting, invigorating tension. Unlike minds produce in collaboration a work which unites their separate individualities. The accidental and mechanical nature of the alliance gives it, paradoxically, a certain biological inevitability, for the opera combines text and music in the way that the dissimilar features and qualities of parents are merged in their child. The cases studied in this book have all revealed the same quarrelsome, biological dialectic— in the relation between da Ponte's libertine cynicism or Schikaneder's extempory clowning and Mozart's musical compassion; or between the disintegrativeness of Wagnerian drama and the gratuitous redemptions of Wagnerian music; or between the classical austerity of Virgil and the episodic exuberance of Berlioz's score; or between the laborious Elizabethan conceits of

Shakespeare's decrepit Falstaff and the Italian melliflu-
ousness of Verdi; or between the riddling, symbol-
haunted intricacy of Hofmannsthal or the preciosity of
Wilde and the bellicose sonority of Strauss.

Words and music are enemies, perpetually jealous of
one another, because each longs for the privileges of
the other while resenting intrusions on its own territory. The aim of music is the dissolution of sense into
sound, the aim of words—as in the non-musical
operas of the third chapter—is to retrieve meaning and
to communicate it, despite the blandishments of
sound. Hence, on the one hand, the habit of those
singers who refuse to enunciate consonants and smear
the text into a vapor trail of seraphic vowel-sounds;
hence, on the other, the method of this book, which
has in part treated the texts in salutary isolation from
music. Words and music are united by antagonism.
Opera is the continuation of their warfare by other
means.

# Selected Bibliography

D'Annunzio, Gabriele. *Il trionfo della morte*. 1896.

———. *Il fuoco*. 1900.

Auden, W. H. "Opera Addict." *Vogue,* vol. CXI, no. 11 (July 1948).

———. with Chester Kallman. *The Magic Flute*. 1957.

———. "The Prince's Dog." In *The Dyer's Hand*. 1962.

———. *Worte und Noten: Rede zur Eröffnung der Salzburger Festspiele 1968*. 1968.

Chesterton, G. K. *Robert Browning*. 1903.

Dali, Salvadore. *The Secret Life of Salvador Dali*. Translated by Haakon M. Chevalier. 1948.

Goethe, Johann Wolfgang. *Der Zauberflöte zweiter Teil. Fragment*. In *Gedenkausgabe der Werke, Briefe und Gespräche*, 6. Edited by Ernest Beutler. 1949.

Hanslick, Eduard. *Vienna's Golden Years of Music 1850–1900*. Translated and edited by Henry Pleasants III. 1950.

Heine, Heinrich. "The French Stage: Confidential Letters addressed to M. August Lewald." In *The Works of Heinrich Heine: Prose Writings,* vol. VII. Translated by C. G. Leland. 1892.

Hofmannsthal, Hugo von. *Ausgewählte Werke in Zwei Banden*. 1957.

Huysmans, Joris-Karl. *A Rebours*. 1884.

Jullian, Philippe. *D'Annunzio*. Translated by Stephen Hardman. 1973.

Kierkegaard, Søren. *Either/Or: A Fragment of Life*. Translated by D. F. and L. M. Swenson. 1944.

Lukács, György. *Studies in European Realism.* Translated by Edith Bone. 1950.

Moore, George. *Avowals.* 1911.

Newman, Ernest. "Richard Strauss and the Music of the Future." In *Musical Studies.* 1905.

———. *Testament of Music.* Edited by Herbert van Thal. 1962.

Nietzsche, Friedrich. *The Birth of Tragedy* and *The Case of Wagner.* Translated by Walter Kaufman. 1967.

Rolland, Romain. *Musiciens d'aujourdhui.* 1908.

Schopenhauer, Arthur. "On the Metaphysics of the Beautiful and Aesthetics." In *Parerga and Paralipomena,* vol. 2. Translated by E. F. J. Payne.

Shaw, George Bernard. *Music in London 1890–1894.* Revised and reprinted. 1932.

———. *The Perfect Wagnerite.* 1898.

———. *Man and Superman.* 1903.

Strauss, Richard. *Briefwechsel mit Hugo von Hofmannsthal.* 1926.

Symons, Arthur. "Ballet, Pantomime, and Poetic Drama." In *The Dome,* no. 1 (1898).

———. *Poems.* 2 volumes. 1901.

———. *Plays, Acting and Music.* 1909.

# Index